St John

~ vices

D1150933

Anti-Semitism and Islamophobia

Anti-semitism and Islamophobia:
Hatreds Old and New in Europe

Matti Bunzl

PRICKLY PARADIGM PRESS
CHICAGO

Prickly Paradigm Press, LLC
5629 South University Avenue
Chicago, IL 60637

www.prickly-paradigm.com

ISBN-13: 978-0-9761475-8-9
LCCN: 2007929752

Printed in the United States of America on acid-free paper.

Table of Contents

Anti-Semitism has been in the news for much of the new millennium. Only a few years ago, it had seemed a faint memory of a distant past. But now, Europe, the cradle of anti-Semitism, appears afflicted again. Newspaper stories relate shocking accounts of individual violence from France to Germany, while commentators speculate on the nature and causes for the reawakened scourge.

In the process, something akin to a debate has developed on this "new" anti-Semitism. On the one hand are what some have called the "alarmists." They tend to see the recent rise in anti-Semitic violence as an immediate and massive threat, not only to Europe's Jews, but to Jews worldwide. This is not really surprising, since anti-Semitism appears to them as a kind of historical constant. Holocaust guilt may have suppressed it somewhat in the last few decades. But now, Israel's policies in the struggle with the Palestinians are giving Europe renewed license to openly despise the Jews. For alarmists, anti-Zionism and anti-Semitism are close to indistinguishable, any critique of the Jewish state carrying potential residues of the longest hatred. What used to come in the garb of extreme right-wing nationalism is thus now often dressed as extreme left-wing anti-colonialism, anti-capitalism, anti-globalism. As a target of derision and violence, Europe's Jews function as a proxy for Israel, the United States, and all the forces of globalization. As such, they are not only victims of militant leftists, but of Islamic radicals as well. Indeed, for most alarmists, the new anti-Semitism is centrally an Islamic phenomenon, spurred by anti-Semitic excesses in the Arab world and transported to Europe by its growing Muslim population. The appeasement of that popula-tion also accounts for what alarmists generally regard as the lackluster response to the anti-Semitic crisis. Europe's governments, they reason, are ready to aban-don their Jewish citizens to preserve a volatile peace. Unsurprisingly, most alarmists can be found on the political Right, where they also tend to support the global policies of the Bush administration. Their commitment to Israel, in turn, is often expressed in support for and trust in the Sharon and Olmert governments.

Their opponents in the debate on the new anti-Semitism tend to be critics of the Israeli and American governments, and they generally make their home on the Left of the political spectrum. In the course of the debate, they have been called "deniers," although the term is rather inaccurate given that none of them actually dispute the reality of anti-Semitism. They do, however, question its current salience. Rejecting the idea that criticism of Israel is inherently anti-Semitic, they discount a whole set of phenomena — pro-Palestinian demonstrations, angry attacks on Israel's government, etc. — alarmists regularly invoke to buttress their case for Europe's anti-Semitism. Instead, they point to the relatively small number of actual incidents of physical violence and emphasize the degree of comfort Jews enjoy across the continent. Deniers do recognize that individual Jews and Jewish institutions have increasingly become victims of abuse. But they tend to see those cases as part of larger formations of violence perpetrated by the extreme right wing against Europe's minorities. On some occasions, Jews may have been assaulted by young Muslims, but mainly, it is Jews and Muslims together who are targeted as Europe's "Others."

Simply put, both sides are wrong. Neither is Europe a haven for a renewed and unbridled anti-Semitism somehow coded into the continent's social DNA, nor can all anti-Semitic incidents be subsumed under a general rubric of right-wing violence. Both explanatory frameworks ultimately falter because of their reliance on overly static views of history. For alarmists, anti-Semitism is an immutable force of history, while deniers see right-wing politics in unchanging terms. What is missing is a recognition of the radical historical transformations in the status and function of European anti-Semitism as well as the right wing's project. So far, the stakes of the debate have prevented us from venturing beyond its terms, blinding us, for example, to the true implications of young Muslim immigrants in the new anti-Semitism. A sober analysis, however, is much needed, not least because the political ramifications of the debate are far-reaching.

The stakes are the future of Europe, particularly as it is coming into being in the countries of the European Union. To think that the EU is ground zero for the resurgence of anti-Semitism is simply misguided. Even more, it has obscured the far more pressing reality of Islamophobia. Whereas traditional anti-Semitism has run its historical course with the supercession of the nation-state, Islamophobia is rapidly emerging as the defining condition of the new Europe. The geopolitical implications of this development are enormous.

Monitoring Anti-Semitism

Nothing exemplifies the debate between alarmists and deniers better than the controversy surrounding the European Monitoring Centre (EUMC), the EU's research institute and think tank on racism and xenophobia. To alarmists, the EUMC became the paradigmatic denier when it suppressed a 2003 report on manifestations of anti-Semitism in the European Union it had commissioned from the Center for Research on Antisemitism at Berlin's Technical University. The report, which was subsequently made available by American Jewish organizations, focused on the first half of 2002 when a widely reported wave of attacks took place in France and Belgium. The Berlin researchers regarded these attacks as a "new development" in that "anti-Semitic offenders" were "in some cases" drawn from "Muslim minorities in Europe — whether they be radical Islamist groups or young males of North African descent." In addition, the report stressed an ostensible connection between anti-Semitism and anti-Zionism, noting the media's use of "anti-Semitic stereotypes in their criticism of Israel" and decrying the frequent occurrence of anti-Semitic agitation in the "extreme left-wing scene." Citing such examples as the juxtaposition of swastikas with Stars of David at far-left demonstrations, the authors suggested that anti-Semitism no longer emanated first and foremost from Europe's right-wing extremists but from an emerging alliance of pro-Palestinian leftists, anti-globalization activists, and Islamists.

The EUMC, which is based in Vienna, regarded the report as an irresponsible indictment of entire populations, especially in its identification of Europe's Muslims as a main source of the new anti-Semitism. Noting that the organization was "not in the business of stigmatizing whole communities on the basis of the actions of racist individuals" and citing the report's "poor quality" and lack of "empirical evidence," the EUMC rejected the findings in November of 2003. At the same time, it vowed to continue research on anti-Semitism and promised publication of a comprehensive report for 2004.

"Manifestations of Antisemitism in the EU 2002 – 2003" was issued by the EUMC in March 2004. The report commenced with a careful delineation that rejected the classification of all hostile acts against Jews as anti-Semitic. Only if Jews were targeted "as Jews" was it legitimate to speak of anti-Semitism. By implication, anti-Zionist attitudes were only anti-Semitic if "Israel is seen as being a representative of 'the Jew.'" What was not to be considered anti-Semitic, therefore, was "hostility towards Israel as 'Israel', i.e. as a country that is criticized for its concrete policies." With this in mind, the EUMC found that the years under investigation saw an increase in anti-Semitic incidents in several European countries, but that "the largest group of the perpetrators... appear[ed] to be young, disaffected white Europeans." In some countries, "young Muslims of North African or Asian extraction" did represent a "further source of anti-semitism." But this finding was immediately relativized. Not only did "traditionally antisemitic groups on the extreme right" play a part in "stirring opinion," but divergent modes of data collection rendered the precise identification of perpetrators itself doubtful. In some countries, "the bulk of evidence [was] from the perceptions of victims." Those were "difficult to verify," thereby casting doubt on victims' frequent classification of perpetrators as "'young Muslims', 'people of North African origin', or 'immigrants.'"

Predictably, the alarmists greeted the report with suspicion. The World Jewish Congress, for example, decried the findings as a "blatant whitewash for the sake of maintaining political correctness." Europe, they implied, was in the thrall of its burgeoning Muslim population whose increasing radicalization was tolerated, even abetted, by European Union actions. "Were the EU to recognize the truth, it would be forced to admit that its own statements and policies had, in no small measure, contributed to the anti-Jewish virus that has infected Europe." What emerged in such comments is a Europe indifferent to, and possibly even complicit in, the resurgence of anti-Semitism. And the EUMC, that quintessential organization of the new Europe, seemed to be its consummate representative.

But it would be wrong to interpret the EUMC's actions in those terms. Like almost all of mainstream Europe, the organization is genuinely appalled by the specter of anti-Semitism. It sees it as Europe's darkest inheritance and regards its transcendence as tantamount to the success of the European experiment. The very project of the EU, in fact, is regarded by many of its greatest champions as nothing if not the antithesis to Nazism and the Holocaust. They see a pluralistic, supra-national Europe as the most potent corrective to the continent's genocidal nationalism.

But if the Holocaust stands at the core of the new Europe, its lessons are seen to extend beyond the specificities of Jewish suffering to include all forms of exclusion and intolerance. It is not insignificant in this regard that the EUMC's full designation is European Monitoring Centre on Racism and Xenophobia. Anti-Semitism is always mentioned as a top priority. But it rarely appears alone, as when the organization defended its decision to suppress the anti-Semitism report by Berlin's Technical University by noting that "the EUMC remains 100% committed to its ongoing research on anti-Semitism and all forms of racism and intolerance."

To see anti-Semitism in line with other forms of racism and intolerance is not the same as to disregard it, even though some alarmists might construe it that way. But it does have crucial implications for one's approach to the problem. For one, it suggests a framework that analogizes different groups on account of their experience of exclusion. For another, it trains the spotlight on a common source of racist and xenophobic animus.

The EUMC followed these very precepts in one of its most characteristic projects. "The Fight against Anti-Semitism and Islamophobia: Bringing Communities together" was an ambitious endeavor undertaken in 2002/03 with the support of the European Commission, the EU's quasi-government. The project's title was programmatic. In three successive meetings, community leaders and social scientists contemplated the situation of Jews and Muslims across Europe and discussed joint strategies for the struggle against racism and xenophobia. The initiative's explicit goal was to "move beyond a single-minded focus on protecting the rights of very specific groups." To stem the division of "people into separate groups, each struggling on their own," EUMC Management Board Chairman Robert Purkiss proposed to "build bridges between our different communities, especially between those that are subjected to a range of hostile acts and discriminatory structures."

Those, Purkiss argued, could be traced to European Christianity:

> Our conceptions of European identity are significant drivers of anti-Semitism and Islamophobia.

One of the similarities between anti-Semitism and Islamophobia is their historical relationship to a Europe perceived as exclusively Christian. Jews have of course suffered the most unspeakable crimes by European Christians. But it is true that *all* other religions, including Judaism and Islam, have been excised from the prevailing understanding of Europe's identity as Christian and white. Both Islam and Judaism have long served as Europe's "other", as a symbol for a distinct culture, religion and ethnicity.

Here, then, is the purest articulation of EUMC's vision. Anti-Semitism does exist at the heart of an exclusionary vision of Europe. But so does Islamophobia. And while Muslims have not suffered the trauma of genocide, their structural position as Other is ultimately analogous to that of Jews. Jews and Muslims thus have a common enemy in a right-wing Christian fundamentalism.

Historical Differences

Politically, EUMC's project of bringing Europe's Jewish and Muslim communities together is entirely commendable. Intellectually, however, it has serious flaws. It is true, of course, that from the vantage point of Christianity, both Judaism and Islam are a certain kind of Other. Theologically and historically, however, the two occupy drastically different positions. The role of Judaism in the genealogy of Christianity makes it much more salient in the Christian imagination, to say nothing about the millennia of active persecution.

But even this critical assessment goes along with EUMC's basic conceit of religion as a relevant, even predominant, factor in the contemporary phenomena of anti-Semitism and Islamophobia. This, however, is highly dubious. After all, Europe's post-Enlightenment trajectory has been shaped overwhelmingly by secular forces — liberalism, nationalism, socialism, fascism — and, if anything, secularism is becoming more, not less, dominant across the continent. To pin the homology of anti-Semitism and Islamophobia on a timeless Christianity is to deny its ever-diminishing relevance.

Anti-Semitism and Islamophobia, then, need to be understood in secular perspective, and that immediately reveals them as time and place specific phenomena. Anti-Semitism, for its part, originated in the late nineteenth century. Both the term and its attendant ideology were the brainchild of German intellectuals who made the exclusion of Jews the cornerstone of a political and cultural movement. Hatred of Jews long preceded this movement, of course. But prior to the modern period, anti-Judaism operated on religious grounds. Persecution was often vicious, but, in theory at least, Jews could overcome their stigma through conversion. What was new about the late nineteenth century's variant of Jew-hatred was its anchoring in the notion of race. A secular concept grounded in modernity's striving toward rational classification, the idea of race gave Jews an immutable biological destiny. All this was connected to the project of nationalism, with the champions of anti-Semitism seeing themselves, first and foremost, as guardians of the ethnically pure nation-state. Given their racial difference, Jews could never belong to this national community, no matter their strivings for cultural assimilation. Jews, in other words, could never become German (or French, or English, etc.).

By contrast, Islamophobia emerged quite recently. It is a phenomenon of the late twentieth and early twenty-first centuries, fueled by geopolitics and unprecedented population movements that have brought millions of Muslims to Europe. A long-standing religious underpinning of Islamophobia could be construed on the basis of theological differences, of course. But the actual debate rarely engages religious questions in any meaningful way. Nor does it turn on the issue of race, although it, too, could be seen as a possible valence. What does stand at the heart of Islamophobic discourse is the question of civilization, the notion that Islam engenders a world view that is fundamentally incompatible with and inferior to Western culture.

As a result, Islamophobic claims are actually quite different from those of modern anti-Semitism. Whereas anti-Semites questioned Jews' fitness for inclusion in the national community, Islamophobes are not particularly worried whether Muslims can be good Germans, Italians, or Danes. Rather, they question whether Muslims can be good Europeans. Islamophobia, in other words, functions less in the interest of national purification than as a means of fortifying Europe.

Organizations like EUMC conceive their struggles against racism and xenophobia as part of one larger battle against intolerance. But such a view obscures the distinctions between different forms of hostility. To argue for the fundamental analogy of anti-Semitism and Islamophobia is misleading, not only historically but also in terms of their contemporary articulations. What we need to attend to is the specifics, which, in contrast to EUMC's assessment, to say nothing of the alarmists' consensus, actually reveal the thorough insignificance at the current time of the modern variant of anti-Semitism.

It may seem shocking to assert the irrelevance of the old anti-Semitism. But consider Europe's realities against the backdrop of anti-Semitism's political project. That project sought to secure the purity of the ethnic nation-state, a venture that has become obsolete in the supranational context of the European Union. There, Jews no longer figure as the principal Other, but as the veritable embodiment of the postnational order. As President of the European Commission, Romano Prodi invoked Europe's Jews in exactly these terms:

> I believe we can learn a lot from the history of the Jews of Europe. In many ways they are the first, the oldest Europeans. We, the new Europeans, are just starting to learn the complex art of living with multiple allegiances — allegiance to our home town, to our own region, to our home country, and now to the European Union. The Jews have been forced to master this art since antiquity. They were both Jewish <u>and</u> Italian, or Jewish <u>and</u> French, Jewish <u>and</u> Spanish, Jewish <u>and</u> Polish, Jewish <u>and</u> German. Proud of their ties with Jewish communities throughout the continent, and equally proud of their bonds with their own country.

Statements like this, and they are legion in the new

Europe, could be, and sometimes are, dismissed as nothing but symbolic window dressing. But their ubiquity does suggest the normalization of the Jewish presence in Europe. Ultimately, Prodi and other European politicians can offer such full-throated affirmations precisely because the sentiment is so utterly uncontroversial. In fact, there is no European party of any significance, and this includes the continent's various extreme right-wing movements, that currently champions a specifically anti-Semitic agenda.

Jewish Exclusions

Let me shine the spotlight for a moment on Austria, which I happen to study in great detail and whose history of anti-Semitism is about as gruesome and shameful as it gets. A brief comparison between the interwar period and the current moment quickly reveals the magnitude in the shift away from political anti-Semitism. In the period before World War II, every major political faction was overtly and programmatically anti-Semitic. The German national parties sought the exclusion of Jews on racial grounds, while the Christian Social factions fought the Jewish presence out of a mixture of religious anti-Judaism and reactionary anti-modernism. Even Socialists (and Communists) regularly deployed anti-Semitism in their critiques of capitalism, notwithstanding the fact that many of their leaders were, in fact, Jews.

To this day, Austria is dominated politically by these three factions. Anti-Semitism, however, has faded from their ideological arsenal. This development is actually quite recent. As late as the 1970s, Austria's Socialist Chancellor Bruno Kreisky famously feuded with Simon Wiesenthal over the latter's efforts to bring Austria's Nazi criminals to justice, and the 1980s witnessed the Christian Social Austrian People's Party's reckless use of anti-Semitism in the presidential campaign of Kurt Waldheim. Most significantly, Austria's right-wing Freedom Party — formed as a successor party to the Union of Independents which had been created as a haven for Austria's former Nazis — centrally deployed anti-Semitism in its efforts to safeguard the country's Germanic character.

By the early 1990s, however, the political tide was turning. As Austria's "Grand Coalition" of Social Democrats and People's Party positioned the country as a possible member of the European Union, they not only purged anti-Semitism from their political repertoire, but began a far-reaching rapprochement with Austria's Jewish community. This process commenced with Austria's official acknowledgment of co-responsibility for the crimes of the Third Reich. It was followed by symbolic gestures like the creation of Vienna's memorial for the Jewish victims of the Holocaust. And it led to a new legal vigilance vis-à-vis Nazism, which, in a complete reversal to the postwar decades when trial after trial of accused war criminals ended in acquittals, resulted in such spectacular cases as that of British writer David Irving, who, in 2006, was sentenced by an Austrian court to three years in prison for Holocaust denial. The same process that made the Austrian state a bulwark against National Socialism also engendered numerous cultural initiatives, including the creation of such institutions as Vienna's Jewish Museum, designed to honor and celebrate Austria's Jewish heritage past and present.

Under the leadership of Jörg Haider, the Freedom Party initially maintained its distance from these developments. The party opposed Austria's membership in the European Union on nationalist grounds and refrained from a full-scale repudiation of anti-Semitism. Haider, in fact, was on record with numerous comments that were easily construed as anti-Semitic or as whitewashing the Nazi past. In the wake of Austria's admission to the EU in 1995, however, the Freedom Party's politics changed. It abandoned its traditional nationalism and even began to court Jews as potential party functionaries. For a while, in fact, Peter Sichrovsky, the son of Holocaust survivors and a prominent member of Vienna's Jewish community, ascended the ranks of the party (not without controversy, however). By the year 2000, when the Freedom Party entered Austria's government in a coalition with the People's Party, Haider was prepared to sign an official "Preamble" that admitted Austria's culpability in the "horrendous crimes of the National Socialist regime." Subsequently, the Freedom Party acceded to an agreement for the compensation of Nazi slave laborers, and Haider, himself, helped negotiate the settlement of restitution for Austria's Jewish community.

It has been argued that none of these actions were genuine and that the Freedom Party continued to be a haven of anti-Semitism. On some level, this could have been true, and several minor spats between Haider and Ariel Muzicant, the head of Vienna's Jewish community, suggested this to be a possibility. But such an interpretation misses the enormous transformation of a party whose historical lineage includes many of history's most vicious anti-Semites along with the German nationalist movement's firm commitment to the exclusion of Jews. For such a party to run Jewish candidates is not an insignificant thing.

Austria's Freedom Party is not alone among Europe's far right-wing movements. While several of them are rooted in traditions of virulent nationalism, none deploy conventional forms of anti-Semitism today.

Consider the case of Jean-Marie Le Pen's National Front in France. As a political movement, its origins lie in the exclusionary nationalism of the late nineteenth century and the fascist strands of the interwar period. Anti-Semitism functioned as the unifying feature in these contexts, designed to integrate the national community across social classes. When Le Pen founded the National Front in 1972, he seemed to tap into this very tradition. Aside from acting as an apologist for the Vichy regime, it was his notorious comments on the Holocaust that cemented his reputation as an unalloyed anti-Semite. In a 1987 interview he spoke about the Nazi gas chambers. Noting that he had neither seen them himself nor devoted "any special study to the subject," he dismissed them as "just a detail in the history of World War II." Le Pen repeated the sentiment over the next years, part of a larger strategy to challenge France's Republican consensus. That strategy also included the identification of some of his political adversaries as Jews, a violation of the neutrality of France's public sphere. Particularly infamous was the 1988 pun on the name of Socialist minister Michel Durafour, rendered by Le Pen as "M. Durafour-Crématoire" (crematory oven).

But Le Pen's discourse has changed. Over the last few years, he has assumed a more moderate posture. On most issues, his position is unaltered. He is still an ultra-nationalist who combines anti-European with anti-American attitudes, and he is still as anti-immigration as he has ever been. But he is less strident. And most noticeably, he is careful to avoid any semblance of anti-Semitism. In fact, Le Pen now protests rather vigorously any accusation that either he or his party are anti-Semitic. "I do not know one person in the National Front who committed even the most minor hostile act against a Jewish person or Jewish property," he noted in a 2002 interview. "As for me, even though I have been accused of anti-Semitism countless times, no one has ever heard me make anti-Semitic statements or engage in anti-Semitic behavior."

As if to underscore the party's new orientation, the National Front, much like Austria's Freedom Party, now runs a Jewish candidate. Sonia Arrouas, who comes from a traditional North African Jewish family, entered Le Pen's circle via his second wife, "some of whose best friends, including myself, are Jews." For some years, Arrouas served as Le Pen's unofficial advisor on Jewish issues. And while she allows that some of Le Pen's old remarks had an anti-Semitic tone, she says that "that was long ago" and that "he has changed his view." The evidence: Le Pen's admiration for the State of Israel and its "policy of defense in the face of the aggression of the Arab world." Add to this his uncompromising position on domestic issues, particularly the status of Islam, and the National Front emerged as a viable political home for a Jew intent to "fight ... for our region, for our security and for our religion." This she did with her candidacy in the 2004 regional elections.

For the leadership of the National Front, such developments are evidence for the fact that "Jews have started to take an interest in our manifesto." Those are the words of Marine Le Pen, the daughter of Jean-Marie Le Pen and a key figure in the movement. She represents the contemporary, "softer" version of a party that has effectively abandoned its anti-Semitic roots. While an overwhelming majority of France's Jews may remain hostile to the National Front, the party's transformation is likely to produce more Jewish candidates in the future, evidence for the normalization of Jewish participation across France's entire political spectrum.

Such a normalization has also occurred in Great Britain. The home of a "gentlemanly" tradition of anti-Semitism, less characterized by violence than subtle exclusion, it has recently marked a watershed: the election of a Jew, Michael Howard, to the leadership of the Conservative Party.

The modern Tories had been founded by Benjamin Disraeli, of course. But it was crucial that this son of Sephardic Jews had been baptized as a child. Even still, he was the occasional object of anti-Jewish derision and when the political moment was opportune, could readily be charged with being unpatriotic. But as a Christian, a political career was at least open to him. Jews, by contrast, were not formally emancipated until 1858, almost 30 years after Catholics. In the decades after emancipation, Jews continued to face various forms of discrimination, the rise of individual Jews to the upper echelons of society notwithstanding. If anything the situation actually deteriorated in the first half of the twentieth century when admission to public schools and elite colleges became restrictive, restaurants and hotels advertised their disinclination to serve Jews, and formal bans were instituted in sporting clubs.

Anti-Semitism declined after World War II. In terms of political participation, Jewish Members of Parliament became commonplace, for example, particularly among the ranks of the Labor Party. In the Conservative Party, however, pre-war sentiments persisted. As the party of social privilege and inherited wealth, it also became the political harbor for British anti-Semitism. Until the 1950s, there had never been a single Jewish MP for the Conservative Party, and by 1970, the number had only reached two. Meanwhile, Jewish Conservatives had trouble getting selected as candidates by local constituency parties. Michael Howard's own political career was stymied by such circumstances. The child of a Romanian-Jewish refugee father and a Welsh-born Eastern European Jewish mother, he was rejected by some 40 constituency parties before finally landing a district in 1982. His background was widely believed to be the reason for the coolness among the party's true-blue selection committees.

But things were already changing. Margaret Thatcher's revolutions were underway, and they extended to the nature of the Conservative Party. Thatcher herself was instrumental in opening the Tories to Jewish participation. Running in the London suburb of Finchley since the late 1950s, she reached out to the many Jewish voters in her district. Upwardly mobile, they, in turn, were attracted to her business approach which stressed independence, self-help, and hard work over traditional status. When Thatcher became Prime Minister, the remaining barriers against Jews quickly fell away. At one point, her cabinet counted five Jewish members, and by 1987, there were sixteen Jewish Tory MPs.

When Howard sought the party leadership in 2003, it was in this thoroughly changed context. By all accounts, his Jewishness was no detriment whatsoever. On the contrary, as his potential rival David Davis suggested prior to the voting, "if anyone notices at all there will be more approvers than disapprovers." Howard's leadership of the Conservative Party was ill-fated, of course, ending in 2005 after his failure to unseat Tony Blair's Labour Government. But it was widely hailed as confirmation for the passing of a genteel anti-Semitism that had been endemic in Great Britain for well over a century.

In the wake of the struggles for Jewish emancipation and the rise of racial anti-Semitism, Jews were targets of political discrimination across Europe. Calls for often violent exclusion were pervasive during the interwar years, and well into the second half of the twentieth century, Jews were marginalized by Europe's political parties, particularly those on the right. Today, such projects are not on any discernable political agenda as Jews participate in European politics across the spectrum. The modern form of anti-Semitism has run its historical course.

Anti-Semitism/Anti-Zionism

This does not mean, however, that we should be blind to the perils of the new anti-Semitism. While the extent of the phenomenon remains in social-scientific dispute, there is little doubt that an increase in anti-Semitic incidents has occurred since 2002 and that many of these, in a departure from traditional patterns of anti-Semitism, have been perpetrated by Muslim youth. Deniers have had trouble grasping the specifics of the current situation in light of their ongoing focus on anti-Semitism as a right-wing phenomenon. Alarmists, meanwhile, have emphasized the Islamic dimension of the new anti-Semitism but offered an implausible explanation that sees it in direct continuity with older forms of Jew-hatred.

The old and new anti-Semitism, however, are radically different phenomena, though maybe not from the point of view of its victims. Violence, after all, is violence; and the concerns of Europe's Jewish communities should give us pause regardless of the source of the threat. But such considerations should not preclude careful political and historical analysis, especially given the flaws in the available explanations of the new anti-Semitism.

What separates the new from the old anti-Semitism is its overarching project. The traditional, modern form of anti-Semitism was designed to effect the exclusion of Jews from the national body. This could take a range of forms, from the polemical assertion of Jews' fundamental incompatibility with the nation to their genocidal eradication. In all the variants of this old anti-Semitism, Jews were construed as intrinsic outsiders to Europe's nation-states, interlopers in a fantasy of ethnic purity.

Insofar as the new anti-Semitism is perpetrated by right-wing extremists, this cultural logic is still at work. But when we approach the phenomenon from its Islamic component, we see a wholly different project. When young, disenfranchised Muslims attack French Jews, they do not do so in the interest of creating an ethnically pure France. Nor are they asserting that French Jews do not belong in Europe. On the contrary, they are attacking Jews precisely because they see them as part of a European hegemony that not only marginalizes them in France, but, from their point of view, also accounts for the suffering of the Palestinians. In the Arab world, Israel, after all, is understood first and foremost as a European colony.

To explain Muslim violence against Europe's Jews as the extension of an anti-colonial struggle is no defense of the phenomenon. But it does make clear how radically different old and new anti-Semitism really are. While the former sought to exclude Jews from the nation-states of Europe, the latter targets Jews precisely because of their Europeanness.

There is a terrible historical irony here. In the conception of Herzl and other Zionist leaders, it was the Jewish state that would resolve the tensions between Europe and the Jews. The Zionist state itself was to be a thoroughly European entity, of course. But those Jews who remained in Europe would also experience a transformation. No longer the stateless parasites despised by the old anti-Semitism, they would receive new respect as members of a viable national community. The existence of Jews in Europe was to be enhanced, in other words, by their connection to a quasi-European nation-state.

Over the decades, Europe's Jewish communities have often seemed like satellites of Israel, in fact, and that may well have mitigated traditional anti-Semitic sentiments. Now, however, it has become a liability as the Zionist promise of Europeanizing the Jews is haunted by its own success. As young Muslims target Jews as expatriates of a colonizing state, they confirm Zionism's ultimate achievement: Europe's Jews have finally become European.

This analysis, then, also speaks to the question of anti-Zionism. Alarmists often focus on the issue in their warnings against the new anti-Semitic threat. But their assertion that anti-Zionism is nothing but a permutation of the old anti-Semitism is plainly false. To be sure, certain ideologies underlying Islamic violence against Europe's Jews do combine opposition to the state of Israel with systemic hostility against all Jews. But on Europe's political spectrum, only a truly lunatic and utterly insignificant right-wing fringe shares this particular set of antipathies.

Much more common is a set of hybrids. Certain elements on the European Left were and are quite demonstrably anti-Zionist, for example. Typically, however, this position, which is usually artic-ulated through a mixture of anti-colonialism, anti-nationalism, and anti-capitalism, also includes resolute opposition to the old anti-Semitism. Soviet-style communism was an example, at least in its early theory, combining a rejection of Jewish national difference with an absolute insistence on assimilation. In the present era, a similar amalgamation of sentiments fuels parts of Europe's anti-globalization movement, whose more official spokespersons never tire in their condem-nation of anti-Semitism, their criticism of Israel's poli-cies notwithstanding.

On the other side, there is a rich tradition, of which Zionism itself is a part, that unites support for a Jewish state with a view of Jews' fundamental incom-patibility with Europe's nations. This anti-Semitic Zionism could often be found among Europe's more centrist Right, where it took the form of Jews' symbolic exclusion on religious grounds. To those who felt that Jews would or should remain aliens in a Christian nation, the existence of Israel gave comfort in the knowledge that, especially after the Holocaust, Jews now had a state of their own. This tradition also accounts for the position of America's religious Right, fervent supporters of Israel who also work for the transformation of the United States into a fundamentalist Christian state.

In one variant or another, some of these positions still exist in today's Europe. But they are completely marginal. The mainstream consensus, articulated by all political parties with any degree of influence, is based neither on anti-Semitism nor on anti-Zionism, but on their conjoined repudiation. In contrast to the interwar years, when many of Europe's parties openly declared their design for the minimization (or worse) of Jewish influence, today's leaders champion the preservation, both of the continent's Jewish communities and the state of Israel. The proliferation of official conferences addressing the new anti-Semitism suggests as much. In the last few years, large-scale events have been organized by the Anti-Defamation League, the Organization for Security and Co-Operation in Europe (two), and the European Union; at each of them, Europe's governments rededicated themselves to the unconditional struggle against anti-Semitism as well as to Israel's right to exist.

And why not? Neither of them are controversial propositions from the vantage point of the new Europe.

Islamophobic Realities

Contrast this consensus with the dynamics around the phenomenon of Islamophobia. Here, Europe speaks with anything but a unified voice. To be sure, the rise in anti-Muslim attacks following the events of September 11, 2001 prompted broad condemnations and led to increased monitoring of Islamphobia's most violent aspects. But the overarching policy thrust has been decidedly more ambiguous, especially on the question of immigration. There, the European Union has been coupling a nominal commitment to integration with efforts at centralization broadly intended to curb migratory movements, particularly, though not exclusively, from the Arab and Islamic world.

Perhaps the most crucial aspect of Islamophobia, however, concerns Turkey's possible membership in the European Union. As early as 1963, the then European Community signed an Association Agreement with Turkey to enhance trade and economic relations and work toward an eventual customs union. After many delays, such a union was finally achieved in 1995. By then, Turkey had also made a formal request for EU membership, which, after the unusually long period of twelve years, did result in the 1999 recognition of Turkey as an applicant country. The latest stage in the process occurred in December 2004, when the EU's heads of state decided on the formal commencement of accession talks, which did, in fact, begin in October of 2005.

Over the decades, a series of recurring concerns have marred Turkey's aspirations for greater involvement in the European project. These centrally include the country's economic status and political situation. There is widespread agreement that Turkey's recognition as an EU applicant country has led to enormous progress in these domains. Inflation has been curtailed and the economy is rapidly modernizing and growing. At the same time, the role of the country's military has been diminishing, while, for the first time in the history of the Turkish nation-state, minorities are accorded a certain degree of respect and a number of crucial rights. Turkey's leadership expects to be rewarded for these reforms with eventual EU membership, and while a number of concerns remain on the table — many having to do with the country's sheer size and overall demographics — the steady support of key figures in the European Union, especially Tony Blair, bodes well for Turkey's aspirations.

But there are also countless detractors. For this highly vocal group, no issue is more troubling than Turkey's Muslim character, the country's long tradition of secularism notwithstanding. Among the most prominent, Valery Giscard d'Estaing — the former President of France and head of the Convention on the Future of Europe, the body charged with drafting a European constitution — has likened Turkey's possible entry into the EU to the end of Europe. Turkey, he asserted in November of 2002, had a "different culture, a different approach, a different way of life." The comment was controversial. But it captured a widespread sentiment, not only among the European Right, that Europe's future would be endangered by the accession of a Muslim country.

Yet again, the Austrian case is instructive. For some time now, Turkey's possible membership in the EU has been a prominent political theme. Whereas anti-Semitism has not played a discernable role in electoral politics in well over a decade, the question of Islam has been gaining importance with each vote. With the decision on accession talks scheduled for later in the year, Turkey, in fact, was the dominant topic in the June 2004 election to the European Parliament.

Predictably, it was Jörg Haider's Freedom Party that put the issue center stage. "Turkey into the EU? Not with me!" was the main slogan of the party's leading candidate, plastered on thousands of billboards across the country. Here is how the party elaborated its position in a pamphlet sent to Vienna's voters:

> Just because 3% of Turkey happen to be in Europe geographically does not mean that Turkey is a European state...
>
> It is a fact that there was no Enlightenment and no Renaissance in Turkey, those bases of European culture that form the standards for all member states of the EU. In addition, one of the most important values of Europeans, tolerance, does not count in Turkey: here, Christians are hassled in any possible way...
>
> Turkey's State Institute for Statistics Forecasts a population of 95 million for the year 2050. The country with the highest population in the EU would then be Islamic!
>
> Not without reason did Libya's head of state Muammar Gadaffi note that Europe would accept an Islamic Trojan horse if Turkey became a member of the EU. This Trojan horse will not only cause social tensions of never anticipated proportions — also the question of Europe's Islamization is being kept quiet by the fanatics for membership. Today, an estimated 15 million Muslims already live in the member states of the EU. Europe can save a lot if it spares itself. Turkey's EU accession would certainly be the end of this community and it would also foil the basic idea of the process of European unification...
>
> The fact that Turkey is part of NATO and has close economic ties with Europe, all that can be no reason to enable Turkey's membership in a union that defines its identity out of a historical tradition.

The virulence of these sentiments may seem surprising. Yet they are entirely within keeping with the Freedom Party's agenda and rhetoric. Indeed, they virtually embody the party's trajectory over the last decade.

When the Freedom Party abandoned its traditional nationalism in the mid-1990s, it embraced a new exclusionary project. Instead of the ethnic community, however, it now cast itself as the protector of Europe. This shift put the spotlight on a novel set of Others. Jews had interfered with the purity of the nation-state; but from the vantage point of a supranational Europe, they were no longer outsiders. Rather, Europe was undermined by such groups as Africans and Asians who quickly emerged as targets for surveillance and exclusion. Most importantly, however, it was Muslims who now appeared as a potential threat.

The 1997 Freedom Party platform made this transformation abundantly clear. In place of obeisance to the (German) nation, the party spoke of a general commitment to German and European history. There was much talk of Europe's common values and heritage, and Judaism's contributions to them were explicitly acknowledged. These European "foundations," however, were "endangered by different streams of thought." The platform identified "radical Islam" as the greatest threat. It was "penetrating Europe" and had to be stopped both at the national and European level.

In terms of policy, this meant a relentless focus on the question of immigration. With slogans like "*Stopp der Überfremdung* [An end to the process of being overrun by foreigners]," the Freedom Party at once generated and appealed to fears of "Islamization." If anything, Jews were constructed as allies in this struggle over Europe's future. "Among my Jewish friends," a prominent Freedom Party politician announced in November of 1999, "there is outrage about the high degree of Islamic presence."

The Freedom Party's agitations had enormous success. Even prior to the party's 2000 entry into Austria's governing coalition, its steady electoral gains forced Social Democrats and the People's Party to severely tighten Austria's immigration laws. The situation did not change significantly in the wake of the party's governance. While internal squabbles led to a string of electoral defeats, the Freedom Party continued to set the political agenda, particularly on issues regarding immigration and the future of the new Europe.

The 2004 EU election was a case in point. In making Turkey's membership the core of its campaign, the Freedom Party not only provoked an often Islamophobic discussion, but effectively forced its competitors to take positions on the politically uncomfortable issue. Indeed, by the time the election neared, the leading candidates of all parties voiced their opposition to Turkey's EU membership. None couched their resistance in the strident terms of the Freedom Party, and the candidates of the Social Democrats and Greens were particularly careful to avoid the semblance of Islamophobia. But Ursula Haubner, the Freedom Party's national chair and Jörg Haider's sister, was still left to gloat that, once again, Austria's political establishment had come around to the Freedom Party's position. "May I remind you that all the others had at least been 'open' to Turkey's accession to the EU."*

---

*In a stunning political development, Austria's Freedom Party split into two factions in April of 2005. The secession was led by Haider himself, who, in the wake of a falling-out with a group of more traditional nationalists, left the Freedom Party to found the Bündnis Zukunft Österreich (Alliance Future Austria). Of the Freedom Party's leading politicians, a large majority followed Haider, including all of the ministers in the governing coalition (which became a coalition between the People's Party and the Alliance Future Austria). Given the ongoing confusion of the situation, it is too early to foresee the long-term effects of the split. A reunification is quite possible (similar developments have taken place in the Freedom Party's past) but so is an end of parliamentary representation, both for the Alliance Future Austria and the rump party that is now the Freedom Party. The general elections of fall 2006 brought some clarification, at least in the short run. While the Freedom Party received 11% of the vote, the Alliance Future Austria came in at slightly over 4% (much of that support coming from Carinthia, the province where Haider has been governor since 1999). In the wake of the elections, both Freedom Party and Alliance Future Austria are represented in parliament, but neither is part of the new governing coalition between Social Democrats and the Christian Social People's Party.

Muslims, Jews, and the Far Right

Once again, the Austrian situation is hardly unique. The continent's other right-wing movements operate with the same political calculus. In that equation, Islam is identified as the preeminent threat to Europe's future. It is a highly focused logic that has transformed earlier modes of exclusion. Those had mobilized a rather amorphous set of antipathies against immigrants and foreigners more generally. Around the mid-1990s, this xenophobic agenda began to give way to a more specifically Islamophobic project. Migrants became Muslims, and Europe's Right wing found its target.

Pim Fortuyn, the late Dutch pundit and politician, was a crucial figure in this development. In the years before his formal entry into politics, he laid the intellectual foundation for the new orientation. Openly gay, Fortuyn was a social progressive who championed an exclusionary agenda in defense of liberalism's foundational principles. His 1997 book *Against the Islamization of Our Culture* was the key text. In it, he identified Islam, which he deemed a "backward" religion, as a corrosive force poised to undermine the accomplishments of Dutch society. In particular, he focused on three areas where the presence of Islam threatened Holland's progressive status quo: the separation of church and state, the relation between the sexes along with the treatment of homosexuals, and the status of children. Islam, Fortuyn argued, had fundamentally different values in regard to these domains. And as a result, it was essentially incompatible with what Fortuyn glossed as "Judeo-Christian humanistic culture." "Christianity and Judaism have gone through the process of enlightenment, making them creative and constructive elements in society," he elaborated in a later interview. "That didn't happen in Islam. There is a tension between the values of modern society and the principles of Islam."

In the late 1990s, Fortuyn became a sensation on the Dutch scene. Intensely charismatic and rhetorically gifted, his controversial mix of liberal, libertarian, and exclusionary positions struck a chord. In 2001, he embarked on a political career, first with the party Livable Netherlands and then with his own List

Pim Fortuyn. His agenda was straightforward: "As far as I am concerned, no Muslim will ever come in." Those who do, he already announced in *Against the Islamization of Our Culture*, "have to conform, and if not, they are not welcome."

Polls prior to the May 2002 national election suggested that Fortuyn's party was in position to become the largest in parliament, he, himself, poised to become prime minister. It did not come to pass. Nine days before the vote, Fortuyn was assassinated by an animal rights activist. His party, for which he served as posthumous candidate, won seventeen percent of the vote. But within a short time it essentially collapsed, having been a reflection of Fortuyn's personality rather than a coherent movement.

Fortuyn's meteoric career may recede into the distant memory of Dutch politics. The political mode he helped introduce, however, has only gained in prominence over the years. No movement makes this clearer than the Flemish Interest. The Belgian party was founded in 2004. But unlike the List Pim Fortuyn which was created ex nihilo, it is the product of a long-standing nationalist tradition similar to the ones that generated Austria's Freedom Party and France's National Front. In 1978, that tradition, which includes the Flemish nationalists who collaborated during the Nazi occupation, spawned the Flemish Block. That party became one of Europe's most successful right-wing movements, commanding up to fifteen percent of the national vote, with close to twenty-five percent in the Flemish part of Belgium. When the Flemish Block was found by the country's court system to "continually incite toward racial discrimination and segregation," it disbanded and resurfaced as the Flemish Interest. The party's leadership and program remained essentially the same.

Nominally, the core issue of the party is the demand for Flemish autonomy. But given the limited public support for the matter, it is always subordinated to a more standard European right-wing agenda. Next to law and order rhetoric and a call for the absolute end of immigration, this program ultimately centers on the question of Islam. Here is how the Flemish Interest frames the issue in its party platform:

> Islam does not know the equality of women and no separation of church and state, and in this way promotes a climate where so-called honor crimes are being committed, where women who are only even rumored to be dishonorable are declared outlaws. Some imams announce that the sharia, the Islamic law, has priority over our laws. Such customs and proclamations are unacceptable in democracy. They clash with European human rights statutes. For us, freedom of expression, tolerance, non-discrimination, and the separation of church and state are fundamental values.

The platform seems to be lifted straight from Pim Fortuyn. But it is actually restrained compared to the comments available by the party's representatives. Filip Dewinter, for one, does not mince words. For the leader of the Flemish Interest, "Islam is now the No. 1 enemy not only of Europe, but of the entire free world." Dewinter is only consistent when he agrees with the assessment that the Flemish Interest is, in fact,

Islamophobic. "Yes," he recently replied to such a question, "we're afraid of Islam. The Islamization of Europe is a frightening thing."

Where do Jews fit in all of this? Fortuyn had invoked a Judeo-Christian humanistic culture in his warnings against the "Islamization" of European society. Dewinter also mobilizes Jews in his Islamophobic rhetoric. In fact, they occupy a privileged position. They are seen as crucial allies in a world historical struggle. Israel stands at the heart of this construction:

> We in Western Europe should realize that our allies are not in the Arab or Muslim world, but rather in Israel. This is not just because we have a common civilization and values, but also to balance out the Islamic forces in the Middle East that are getting stronger. The State of Israel is a sort of outpost for our Western society, an outpost of democracy, of freedom of speech, of protecting common values within a hostile environment.

Dewinter's admiration for Israel is probably the least surprising aspect of his philo-Semitism. What is more remarkable given the history of the Flemish Interest is his affection for the Jews of Belgium, many of whom, especially in Antwerp, are ultra-orthodox and as such the traditional bête noire of the right-wing imagination. But Dewinter enthuses that "Jews integrate into the surrounding society without any problem. They don't bother anyone. They respect the law." Not even their overt difference disturbs him, to say nothing of their social structure organized as it is around the different valuation of the sexes. "Maybe they have a few habits that seem a bit strange to us, but they do not oppose our way of life."

Belgian Jews are evidently beginning to reciprocate these overtures. It is not just the pro-Israel and pro-Jewish rhetoric that attracts them to the Flemish Interest. They are also taking note of Dewinter's aggressive distancing from the party's association with Nazism past and present. Most importantly, however, a growing number see the Flemish Interest as their main defender against the perceived threat of Muslim violence. The events of 2002 play a key role in this regard. For the then Flemish Block, the attacks against Jews were grist for the mills, ostensibly confirming their warnings of the imminent dangers emanating from Belgium's Muslims. Many Jews experienced the resulting statements as the only decisive reaction to the crisis. As one ultra-orthodox Jew put it in a 2003 interview, "At that time, the only ones who consistently supported us were the *Vlaams Blok* [the Flemish Block]. No one else cared that Jews were being beaten up and degraded right inside Antwerp."

Not too long ago, Jewish votes for the Flemish Block/Flemish Interest were utterly inconceivable. Today, they are commonplace. And while the numbers are still small, they are clearly growing. Estimates based on the results of polling stations in heavily Jewish precincts suggest that over ten percent of Antwerp's Jews cast their ballots for the party in recent elections. Other calculations project the Jewish support for the Flemish Interest as high as fifteen percent.

The same dynamic is in evidence in France where the National Front used to be anathema to the country's Jews. Now, the party has become a plausible option. Again, the numbers are quite small. But as the 2002 presidential election demonstrated, there is a growing pool of support, especially among the Jewish communities in the south and the Parisian suburbs, the regions where Jews live among sizable Muslim populations. Even before Le Pen's startling success in the election — he came in second and advanced to a runoff with Jacques Chirac — Roger Cuikerman, the President of the Representative Council of Jewish Organizations in France, acknowledged the changed situation. While calling Le Pen the "king of anti-Semitism and our great enemy," he also suggested that the National Front and the Jews of France did share a "common interest." Elaborating in the wake of Le Pen's triumph, Cuikerman explained that "Le Pen's success is a message to Muslims to keep quiet, because he is known as someone who has always been opposed to Muslim immigration." Minimally, he added, it would force the next government to "put great emphasis on the struggle against [all forms of] violence... including violent anti-Semitism."

The National Front is clearly pleased with this rapprochement. As Marine Le Pen put it, "The Jews have understood who is truly responsible for anti-Semitism." With that, "they perceive us differently. The misunderstandings of the past are fading." From the Jewish point of view, the alliance may be grudging. But the National Front's promise of a struggle against the "Islamization of France" is beginning to resonate. Just like France's population at large, the Jewish community has become receptive to the politics of Islamophobia.

European Futures

All over Europe, immigration, the status of Islam, and the possibility of Turkey's EU membership are central topics of political debate. More often than not, the terms are dictated by the far Right. And the eventual outcome, on Turkey's accession, for example, is far from certain. Islamophobia, in this sense, is a genuine political issue, part of a wide-open debate on the future of the Muslim presence in Europe.

Anti-Semitism, by contrast, is not. This is not to downplay the dangers of the new anti-Semitism, but to recognize that it operates on a completely different level. There simply is no debate on the legitimacy of the Jewish presence in Europe, unless we count Ariel Sharon's July 2004 plea that the Jews of France leave for Israel immediately. All factions of Europe's political spectrum, from far Left to far Right, are united in their commitment to the future of European Jewry.

There is some validity to the EUMC's analogy between anti-Semitism and Islamophobia, of course. Both, after all, are exclusionary ideologies mobilized in the interest of collective engineering. But the similarities end there. While anti-Semitism emerged in the late nineteenth century and had its greatest influence in the early twentieth century, Islamophobia is a phenomenon of the current age. And while anti-Semitism was designed to protect the purity of the ethnic nation-state, Islamophobia is marshaled to safeguard the future of European civilization. The fact that an extreme right-wing fringe holds both ideologies simultaneously cannot obscure these fundamental distinctions.

Europe needs to address the problem of anti-Semitism, and it must do so on its own terms and in recognition of its particular history. Much more pressing, however, is the issue of Islamophobia, both in terms of Europe's future and the geopolitical situation at large. As the European Union is stumbling toward a more unified future, a number of approaches to Islam have emerged. One is the American model, with its constitution beyond ethnic and religious principles and its civic encouragement of and respect for multiculturalism. Another is the French concept of *laïcité*, which, in demanding cultural homogeneity, at least affirms Muslims' ability to become fully French (and hence European).

But there are also the more sinister visions, associated with right-wing figures from Pim Fortuyn to Jean-Marie Le Pen. To them, Muslims are bearers of a fundamentally distinct culture and hence essentially unassimilable. To preserve its character and greatness, Europe, they hold, has to erect a barrier, whether against Turkey's membership in the EU or the additional influx of immigrants from North Africa and the Middle East. Support for this Islamophobic position is growing, and were it to prevail, the geopolitical consequences would be enormous. Not only would it halt the promising reforms in Turkey, but it would likely lead to a new radicalization, both in Europe and across the Islamic world, where more and more young Muslims would become holy warriors in an endless clash of civilizations. A consequent rise in anti-Semitism would then be our smallest problem.

Reflections on Anti-Semitism and Islamophobia

Dan Diner
Leipzig University/Hebrew University

In his piece on anti-Semitism and Islamophobia in Europe, Matti Bunzl makes an interesting observation by assigning modern virulent hatred of the Jews its historical locus in the classic nation-state of the late nineteenth and early twentieth century, while seeing Islamophobic reaction as a phenomenon within the "Europeanizing" of Europe in recent years. While the Jews are viewed as the significant Others in the homogenizing, primarily ethnic construction of the nation-state in Europe's past, the Muslims and Islam take on an analogous importance in the context of European unification as it deepens today.

This concept is certainly correct on a phenomenological level. One may note reactions hostile to the Jews here and there nowadays, but it is difficult to contend that this is a serious current of virulent Jew-hatred. By contrast, fairly widespread animosity toward Muslims is on the increase. It is hard to determine whether these reactions are solely xenophobic in nature, and are directed against Muslims principally as strangers, as alien Others, as outsiders; or that more is involved — such as evoking deep strands of tradition against Islam as such, in part anchored in Christian roots, however secularized. Probably both elements are present, though there are various intermediary stages between an anti-Muslim xenophobia and a full-blown Islamophobia that is in essence ideological.

The distinction between a more common animosity toward the Others, and a highly aggregated animus anchored in a world view of the Other, is the main point I would like to touch on in relation to Matti Bunzl's piece. And I would like to address this using the same object he discusses so impressively. It begins with the concepts employed here and their history. A historian finds it important to note when concepts emerge and what use is made of them in that envelope of time and space. When the concept of anti-Semitism first surfaced in Europe in the 1870s, it was used as a term of self-reference by those who wanted to promote a new understanding of animosity toward the Jews. The key concept of modern Judeophobia was no longer religious alone at its core, and not what increasingly would take center stage as the concept of race. Rather, at its hub were conceptions that are better understood as *reactions* to an intensifying modernity and the changes and convulsions that were accompanying it. Hatred toward the Jews that sees itself as anti-Semitism reacts less to what later is considered an *ethnic* attribute and marking. Paradoxically, it is responding far more to what appears hidden to the anti-Semitic gaze, a purported *invisible presence* of the Jews. The trope or figure of power thrusts itself into the center of the conception of anti-Semitism. In this sense, anti-Semitism is not some kind of prejudice toward Jews — an animosity toward the stranger oriented specifically to Jews and their external appearance. Rather, it is a *weltanschauung*, a world view — or more precisely, an explanation of how the world works — beholden in significant measure to notions of a secret conspiracy.

The conspiracy in turn is considered the imaging of abstractions emanating from modernity about a highly complex life world which is not understood. For anti-Semites, the actual problem is not the Jew openly espousing his or her ancestral faith, even though such anti-Semites will tend to despise that Jewish faith, with an animus against Jewish religion on the basis of a secularized Christian tradition. It is likewise not the "ethnic" Jew, that individual of Jewish origin who — due to his or her appearance and lifestyle — is perhaps viewed with disgust by the anti-Semite. Rather, it is the Jew scheming in the dark, or the Jew who is thought to be such a schemer. The core figure on the stage of the anti-Semitic world view is not the visible Jew but the sinister *invisible* Jew.

How does this relate to the phenomenon of Islamophobia? In terms of the history of ideas and concepts, Islamophobia is a quite recent word. Generally, it appears connected rhetorically with the term anti-Semitism. A kind of analogy is thus invoked or suggested. But unlike anti-Semitism in its discursive provenance, Islamophobia is not a self-attribution of those who, for whatever motives, dislike Muslims, or specifically Muslims in Europe. The fact that the appellation stems from others and is not a self-designation can suggest a substantial difference between modern animosity toward the Jews and the analogous phenomenon toward the Muslims, though it is not necessarily so. In addition, open anti-Semitism in the wake of the Holocaust has become harder to profess. Rather, anti-Semites now tend to deny that they are anti-Semitic.

On the other hand, when it comes to Muslims, it's easy to raise the temperature, for the simple fact that most Muslims resident in Europe are primarily emigrants — persons who, largely for social reasons, find it hard to integrate, or for whom integration is made difficult by others. The boundaries blur and turn fuzzy between the xenophobia mentioned above and an *ideologically grounded animosity* toward Muslims — namely Islamophobia — seen as an analogue of anti-Semitism.

There are both similarities and differences between anti-Semitism and Islamophobia. These similarities and differences are less between anti-Semitism and Islamophobia as such and more connected with *reactions* to Jews and Muslims. For Jews, this is concentrated more in the past; for Muslims, it is in the present. The ritual slaughter of Jewish kosher ritual is only one example in a whole bundle of problems, though certainly a central one. It is not surprising when compatibility with indigenous culture condenses precisely at the point of such ritual questions. In that form one can recognize the great questions of passive and active integration. They tend to incline towards a politico-theological direction.

In view of Western, i.e. Christian, secular modernity, what then do Judaism and Islam have in common? And what separates them? Common to both is that they are religions of the Law. In the era of emancipation, Judaism faced problems not so very dissimilar from those which Muslims confront today in Europe. It was a time when the Jews in Western and Central Europe were challenged to transform their all-embracing religion of the Law into a *confessio*, into mere faith or religious affiliation. It was the process of transforming Judaism into a *confessio*, its "Protestantization" so to speak, or its privatization, that rendered full civil equality on the basis of citizenship possible. For the Jews, this transformation was accompanied by the conversion of their religious corpus — and their identity. This transformation of the Jews was facilitated by the fact that Jews in the diaspora were quite familiar with a doctrine of separation between state power and the sphere of faith, as enshrined in the central Aramaic dictum in Jewish law: *dina demalkhuta dina* (the law is the law of the land). That was similar to the fundamental principle in Christianity of giving unto Caesar what is his, and unto the Lord what is his. So Jewish law had to comply with the law of the respective land of sojourn and accept its primacy, and to do so in numerous spheres.

In contrast with diasporic Judaism in its Babylonian tradition, Islam knows no such separation. All spheres are permeated by the divine Law. In principle, Islam is a political religion. This gives rise to certain difficulties, especially when it is a matter in the West of turning an all-compassing religion into a *confessio*. And here the differences between Europe and the United States are striking. While religion in the U.S. is part of civil culture (even if, in terms of institutions, the division between church and state, and the sphere of politics in this formal sense, is absolute and carefully monitored), in Europe the emblems of participation in the commonwealth move more toward adaptation and accommodation. The neutralization of one's origin that occurs in the U.S. has no analogue in Europe, where a more or less secular belonging is imbued with a cultural tinge. It is not easy to acquire these elements of tradition as a prerequisite for participating in the political community, and to shed one's own traditional elements in the process.

The equality of the emancipation spawned modern anti-Semitism in its backwash. Equality, as contrasted with the society of estates in pre-modernity, creates an ensemble of nearness that in turn tends to galvanize the emergence of new difference. Muslims today, like Jews in the past, face the task of transforming their all-encompassing religion into a *confessio*, an abstract faith community among other faith communities. This is a lengthy and painful process. It is rendered even more difficult because it is now accompanied by an Islamophobic reaction in the surrounding society. Only the future will show whether this Islamophobia is by and large a xenophobic behavior or a binary construction of the Other, which is then further ideologized beyond the mere dimension of difference. By that time, it is quite possible that secularized Christian culture in Europe will have begun to recall its own sacred elements, which were jettisoned under the impress of secularization. Such a process of resacralizing culture could lead to a circumstance where both Jews and Muslims are marked as Others: Jews, who, by the very fact of their emancipation, to a certain degree, brought about a transformation of the Christian in a secular direction, as we know from the classic debates between Feuerbach, Marx and Bruno Bauer; and Muslims, who later, over a long period of this transformation of the Christian state, came to enter the European cultural space. When the political commonwealth of the Europeans begins to recall its Christian roots, anti-Semitism in its classic form and Islamophobia as an ideology will come close, and indeed become similar. That, of course, we can hope will not happen.

A Contradiction in "the New Europe"

Brian Klug
St. Benet's Hall, Oxford

There is much in Matti Bunzl's bold and stimulating essay with which I agree. He is right, in my view, to reject the position advanced by the "alarmists," who see a "new" anti-Semitism that is ultimately the return of the "old" in a different guise and who regard Europe as awash with hatred of Jews. Equally, he is right to repudiate the "deniers" for whom anti-Semitism is a right-wing preserve and who tend to play down evidence of anti-Jewish hostility in other quarters (although I am not sure that deniers are as legion as alarmists). I take his point that it is wrong to treat anti-Semitism and Islamophobia as if they were merely two variations on the common theme of bigotry (although I think they might be more analogous than he supposes). And I agree that, as things stand today, Islamophobia is a "far more pressing reality" for "the new Europe."

Bunzl's essay could have been titled "Whither Europe?" (or "Whither the European Union"?), and one of the principal merits of his essay, on my reading, is that he brings to light a hidden contradiction within the supranational idea of "the new Europe." On the one hand, there is the vision of the EU as the "antithesis to Nazism and the Holocaust." As such, the EU is a project within a project; for, if "the Holocaust stands at the core of the new Europe," it also sparked the post-war UN Charter and Universal Declaration of Human Rights. On the other hand, "Islamophobia is rapidly emerging as the defining condition of the new Europe." Putting it crudely, Europe is torn between a *universal* and a *particular* view of itself. Bunzl's essay is a political wake-up call for those of us who wish to resolve the contradiction in favour of the former. With this in mind, he seeks to replace fuzzy, well-meaning thinking about anti-Semitism and Islamophobia with "sober analysis," beginning with the clarification of key terms.

It is in this spirit that I want to offer an alternative to Bunzl's account of the meaning of the term "anti-Semitism." There is a certain tension between how he *defines* the word and the way he *uses* it. Moreover, while I entirely agree that the "old" and "new" anti-Semitism are "radically different phenomena," I would differentiate them differently. The alternative account that I shall offer is intended as a friendly amendment which, while leaving the crux of his overall argument intact, clears up certain points in his essay.

For the most part, when Bunzl uses the word "anti-Semitism" without a qualifier, he means "old" as distinct from "new." (For "old," he sometimes substitutes "traditional" or "modern"; at one point he refers, paradoxically, to "the traditional, modern form of anti-Semitism." When he says that "the modern form of anti-Semitism has run its historical course," he means the same as when he says that "traditional anti-Semitism has run its historical course." This is a little confusing, but it is not confused.) Anti-Semitism (the "old" variety), he tells us, "originated in the late nineteenth century." It entailed a racist ideology and it had a specific "political project," namely, "to secure the purity of the ethnic nation-state." So, on Bunzl's account, anti-Semitism is inseparable — conceptually and historically — from (ethnic) nationalism.

Now, it is true that the term "*Antisemitismus*" was coined (by Wilhelm Marr in 1879) in connection with such a project and that it denoted a specifically *racial* view of Jews. It does not follow, however, that this is integral to the meaning of the word today. (A fact of life about words is that once they enter the language they go their own way.) Bunzl himself, when discussing the Austrian context in the interwar period, remarks, "Even Socialists (and Communists) regularly deployed anti-Semitism in their critiques of capitalism...." (This was not peculiar to Austria, nor to this period, nor was it confined to marginal figures on the Left. "The Jew is the enemy of humankind," wrote Pierre-Joseph Proudhon, the nineteenth century French utopian Socialist. "The race must either be sent back to Asia or exterminated." Mikhail Bakunin, the Russian revolutionary anarchist and Proudhon's contemporary, held that "the whole Jewish world" was "one exploiting sect, one people of leeches, one single devouring parasite".) Now, critiques of capitalism can also be found on the far Right. But, presumably, it is not Bunzl's view that anti-capitalist critiques *on the Left* were part and parcel of the project of creating a racially pure nation-state.

Bunzl's own remark about anti-Semitism in the Austrian context suggests that there might be a phenomenon which, while it has functioned as part of a racial national project, can function in other ways too. Indeed, there is. Although the nineteenth century German political anti-Semites transformed traditional *Judenhass* (hatred of Jews) by secularizing and racializing it, simultaneously they preserved (a version of) the figure of "the Jew": the power-grabbing, money-grubbing, menacing character that haunts the folklore and fairytales of Christian Europe down the centuries. They carried this figure forward at the very nucleus of their ideology: the "Semite" of "anti-Semitism" is the *Jude* of *Judenhass* in modern dress. The term "anti-Semitism," in its ordinary employment today, connotes this figure, wherever it appears: whether on the Right or the Left, and whether discourse is religious or secular.

Accordingly, the EUMC 2004 report defines anti-Semitism as an act or attitude based on "the stereotypical construction of 'the Jew.'" In unpacking this stereotype, the authors draw on a study of Nazi literature; but only for the *characterization* — not the (biological) *racialization* — it contains. And when explaining "the core of antisemitism," they refer to the perception of "the Jew" as a "social subject," not a *racial* subject.

Although early on in his essay Bunzl describes the EUMC definition as "a careful delineation," he does not appear to incorporate it into his analysis. It is open to him, of course, to use the word differently. But then he owes us a word for a phenomenon that, moreover, largely drops out of the picture with his division of anti-Semitism into "old" and "new." When he argues that the former has "run its historical course," what he is really saying is that the project of creating an ethnically pure nation-state is dead. That's as may be. But the figure of "the Jew" is still alive and kicking in various nooks and crannies of European culture. And the most natural word for this (old) phenomenon is "anti-Semitism."

If Bunzl thinks that the *old* anti-Semitism is extinct, he nonetheless cautions that "we should not be blind to the perils" of the *new*. (I take it that he is reiterating this point at the end of his essay when he remarks that Europe "needs to address the problem of anti-Semitism": that is, the problem posed by the "new".) Describing the sea-change that has occurred in the status of Jews in Europe since World War II, he sums things up in a striking aperçu that captures the heart of what he sees as the "new" anti-Semitism: "As young Muslims target Jews as expatriates of a colonizing state, they confirm Zionism's ultimate achievement:

Europe's Jews have finally become European." Seen in this light, "new" anti-Semitism is the other side of the coin to Islamophobia: if the latter "functions... as a means of fortifying Europe" against the Other of Islam, the former represents a reaction by the Islamic Other against European hegemony. (Which, as Bunzl emphasizes, is not to *defend* hostility towards Jews.)

I find this analysis illuminating, although I suspect that the story that needs to be told about the perceptions of "young Muslims" who "target Jews" is more complex. It needs to be adjusted according to national — even local — context. Furthermore, even if it is true that in "the Arab world" Israel is seen "as a European colony," I am not sure about the importance of its (perceived) Europeanness. For some, the mere negative fact that the state is *not* Arab (or perhaps not Muslim) might be sufficiently egregious; for others, it is Israel's presence and conduct in the Occupied Territories that matters. The waters are muddied, moreover, by the extent to which old European anti-Semitic canards, along with tracts like the *Protocols of the Elders of Zion*, have entered anti-Zionist polemics. Nevertheless, a prejudice against Jews that derives from hostility to Israel ("new" anti-Semitism) is, as Bunzl states, "radically different" from hostility to Israel that derives from a prejudice against Jews ("old" anti-Semitism); as this contradistinction shows, they are, in a way, opposites. (Which is why it is unfortunate that the *new* kind of hostility towards Jews is being called *anti-Semitism*; but no Canute can stem the tide of language.)

In the concluding section of his essay, Bunzl warns that the terms of the debate about Europe's future tend to be "dictated by the far Right." This prompts the thought that the contemporary debate over the integrity of European civilization is not, perhaps, quite as different as Bunzl suggests from the debate in the past over the purity of the nation-state. Consider the following remark:

> It is only when [he] insists upon posing as a European, and being judged as a European, that one realises what an obnoxious creature he is, and how utterly out of place in a European country and in European society.

The author is not, as Bunzl's essay perhaps predicts, a twenty-first century Islamophobe. He is Joseph Banister, an Englishman, writing in 1901 about the Jews (*England under the Jews*).

Comment on Bunzl

Paul A. Silverstein
Reed College

Matti Bunzl has authored a stimulating essay which takes on one of the most pressing predicaments of European modernity: the tensions within liberalism between universalist norms of toleration and particularist limits of state sovereignty. Bunzl's examination of the parallel, yet historically divergent discriminatory practices of anti-Semitism and Islamophobia in the New Europe challenges historians to ground their general understandings of intolerance in the particular histories and experiences of Muslim and Jews in Europe. Yet, his essay also points to the present political climate where discourses of historical particularism can ideologically bolster assertions of ethnic exceptionalism and justify state policies of exclusion. In what follows, I explore such tensions.

Colonialism and After: For Muslims in Europe, unlike for Jews, the key historical experience — and one which Bunzl arguably underemphasizes — is that of colonialism. During both the pre-colonial past and the postcolonial present, European Muslims were treated as outsiders, presumed to be fundamentally linked to extra-European Muslim states (an Islamic "civilization"). Colonialism effectively eliminated this Islamic outside, subordinating the southern and eastern shores of the Mediterranean to European rule in the form of settler colonies, mandates, and protectorates. In the French colonies of North Africa and the Levant, a racial order prevailed. Muslims were excluded from full citizenship given their purported submission to Islamic legal regimes and modes of authority. However, in the wake of World War II, Muslims were tentatively assimilated as subordinate, albeit suspect, subjects — as lesser insiders and potential French citizens.

Decolonization simultaneously blocked this process of incorporation (insofar as it established independent states to whom Muslims' citizenship reverted) and contributed to the creation of multi-generational communities of Muslim immigrants in the metropole. In general, decolonization contributed to the progressive Europeanization of former imperial European states. However, the former colonies remained largely within their former colonizers' spheres of economic, political, and cultural influence, as younger siblings and potential allies in Cold War geopolitics. It was only in the wake of the 1973 Arab-Israeli War and oil embargo, the 1979 Iranian revolution and hostage crisis, and the escalation of the Lebanese civil war following the 1982 Israeli invasion, that Islam was re-positioned as an existential threat to the West, and Muslim residents of Europe subjected to xenophobia as "Muslims" (as opposed to, say, immigrant workers in competition with nationals for jobs). As Bunzl rightly suggests, the Europeanization of Europe and the Islamization of European Muslims went hand in hand.

And yet, in spite of European integration, the national and racial reason of colonialism has not fully disappeared, and in many ways has been re-created in the postcolonial present. More than anything, the "war on terror," pursued by European states since the 1980s and bolstered after the September 11th attacks, has resulted in the systematic racial profiling which targets Muslims as visible and suspect subjects, singling them out by how they look, what they wear, and where they live. In France, the peripheral housing projects where many Muslims reside have become veritable militarized zones, with young North African and Black residents subject to daily harassment from security forces, with their congregation in various public areas (including the basements and entryways of their own buildings) criminalized.

In their experiences of institutionalized discrimination, French Muslim men and women do not, pace Bunzl, face the nation as superceded. They precisely feel excluded from a nation whose citizenship they nominally hold, but whose recent laws — including the banning of *hijab*, or the requirement that the "positive aspects" of colonialism must be taught in public schools — appear to disproportionately victimize them. And they live this exclusion as *racial*, as occurring at the level of their bodies in the forms of physical violence and harassment. They experienced the racial and spatial "apartheid" — to borrow Balibar's assessment — which they live as but a post-colonial continuation of the colonial forms of exclusion and violence which their parents experience, and they view their own struggle for rights and respect as one and the same as that of their parents.

Moreover, they present their current condition as consonant with that of other oppressed, racialized groups: be they African Americans in the United States or Palestinians in the Occupied Territories. Insofar as Israel appears to many European Muslims as an ongoing colonial apartheid state, it is not at all surprising that they should feel some level of solidarity with the Palestinian plight — not because of any transnational ethnic or religious unity, but simply out of a similarity of perceived circumstances. And when this identification occurs in a European context of apparent double standards — where oblique anti-Semitic remarks are criminalized while blatantly Islamophobic cartoons are protected under freedom of speech laws, and where toleration of Jewish (but not Muslim) difference becomes the *sine qua non* of Europeanness — it is likewise not surprising that these young Muslims might regard Jews as fully integrated

European insiders and indeed as iconic of all which is intolerable in their own lives.

The Pernicious Politics of Difference: And yet insisting on the particular history of discrimination faced by European Muslims — identifying the precise colonial genealogy of Islamophobia, as I, inspired by Bunzl's essay, have just done — has a very real ethical danger. For the politics of Muslim difference is, in the present climate, ultimately a politics of exclusion. The "alarmist"/"denier" debate, which Bunzl details in the opening pages of his essay, marks more an ideological quarrel than a differential assessment of the empirical world of anti-Semitism and Islamophobia. Both groups (with certain extremist exceptions) generally concur that a rise in reported incidents of violence against Jewish individuals and property in Europe occurred during the early years of the new millennium, and that many, though not necessarily the majority, of such attacks have been perpetrated by young European Muslims. The deniers do not deny the seriousness of such attacks. And the alarmists are not particularly alarmed about an overall existential threat to European Jewry as such.

Rather, the alarmists are explicitly alarmed by what they insist is a fundamental incompatibility between Islam and Europe, and particularly with Europe's post-war norms of secularism and democracy. They fear the progressive "Islamization" of Europe, by the creation of what Bat Ye'or has termed a "Eurabia" in which Christians and Jews will be eventually reduced to a state of "dhimmitude," of forced submission. For alarmists, anti-Semitic attacks by Muslims demonstrate

European Muslims' incapability of living in a religiously tolerant society, serve as an index of the Muslim community's inherently fundamentalist tenor, and justify a heightened "war on terror." Such a position not only sidelines a recognition of the discrimination against Muslims in Europe, but tends to be Islamophobic in and of itself.

Moreover, such alarmism bolsters a defense of Jewish exceptionalism, of Jews' privileged insider status as European cosmopolitans. In France, alarmism about a rising Muslim anti-Semitism responded as much to reports of anti-Semitic attacks as to growing state efforts to incorporate Muslims via a French Council of the Muslim Faith (CFCM), an elected body designed explicitly, in the words of interior minister Nicolas Sarkozy, to "bring Islam to the table of the Republic." The CFCM was specifically modeled on the Representative Council of Jewish Institutions of France (CRIF) which had successfully served as an interlocutor between the heterogeneous French Jewish community and the state since the end of World War II. In their writings, French alarmists have consistently rejected depictions of the French Jewish and Muslim "communities" as commensurable groups — or of anti-Semitism and Islamophobia as equivalent hatreds — and have argued that Muslim immigrants are incapable of full integration into the French Republic. In other words, alarmists effectively reject the possibility that Muslims, like Jews, can become insiders to France or Europe more broadly.

More precisely, such a defense of Jews' exceptional incorporation in Europe is a claim to an ownership of victimhood. Alarmists tend to write as if there exists a zero-sum game of suffering, as if the recognition of Islamophobia will somehow dilute a narrative of Jewish persecution that, in certain versions, justified the creation of the state of Israel and its continued existence. Alarmists seem to be alarmed that an increased attention to European Muslim (or Palestinian) discrimination will break the Jewish monopoly on victimization, and hence threaten the recognized need for a Jewish state. In other words, they have a political interest in insisting on the ongoing threat of anti-Semitism, and in linking Muslim anti-Semitism in Europe and the Middle East to the Palestinian struggle.

In the end, then, the discussion of anti-Semitism and Islamophobia in Europe is inextricably caught up in the politics of the Israeli/Palestinian conflict, and the European debate has become a site where different positions on the balance of Israeli security and Palestinian rights are being articulated by proxy. Beyond their pernicious equation of anti-Zionism and anti-Semitism, alarmists consistently discredit the Palestinian struggle by equating "suicide bombings" with Nazi genocide within a continuity of anti-Semitism. Their alarm about the reported spike in anti-Semitic attacks is thus less a concern about Europe's Diaspora Jews than about the lack of support for Israeli state policies by European governments.

It is impossible to over-emphasize the stakes of combating such alarmist claims to ethnic exceptionalism. As historians and anthropologists, we are trained to separate out the historical records into precise genealogies, to insist on cultural complexity in the face of universalizing theories of the human experience. And, yet, such a methodology of disaggregation can prove pernicious. As dissimilar as anti-Semitism and Islamophobia may be as historical structures of intolerance, we must be careful that our insistence on such particularities does not blind us to the ways that they are experienced, in the present, as equally violent modes of exclusion. Whatever its shortfalls, the EUMC's project of reading anti-Semitism and Islamophobia (and racism, more broadly) within a single rubric succeeds in insisting that both Muslims and Jews are susceptible qua Europeans. We must insist that Jews and Muslims are ultimately commensurable folk, that they both can be, and often are, victims and victimizers. Otherwise, what is at risk is not only the non-recognition and perpetuation of Muslim suffering, but the exacerbation of an Islamophobic "war on terror" which threatens, as Bunzl warns, to turn the "clash of civilizations" into a self-fulfilling prophecy.

Power and the Politics of Prejudice

Adam Sutcliffe
King's College London

The torture and murder of Ilan Halimi, a Jewish
mobile phone salesman, in the northern suburbs of
Paris in February 2006 underscored the enduring reality of European anti-Semitism. However, contrary to
the perception of many in the United States, the continent is far from being overwhelmed by a resurgence of
ancient hatreds. French Jews are for the most part
comfortably settled in France: levels of emigration
remain very low, notwithstanding much encouragement to move to Israel, and a petition that circulated in
Los Angeles after Halimi's murder urging that Jews

who felt unsafe in France should be welcomed in America. Despite renewed political instability and disillusionment in much of Central and Eastern Europe, anti-Semitism there seems less serious than in the West. The authoritative comparative database of the Stephen Roth Institute for the Study of Contemporary Antisemitism and Racism at Tel Aviv University places the United Kingdom, surprisingly perhaps, at the top of the table of "major violent antisemitic incidents" in 2005, with 89 such incidents recorded. France is second, with 65, and third, perhaps even more surprisingly, is Canada, with 44. Neither the frequency nor the global distribution of these anti-Semitic attacks suggest a reprise of the 1930s.

European governments take anti-Semitism very seriously. The French political response to Halimi's kidnapping and murder was swift and vigorous, as was the reaction to a spate of cemetery desecrations in 2004. In Britain the "Report of All-Party Parliamentary Inquiry into Antisemitism" has recently been published (September 2006) with several recommendations to further improve police and government handling of anti-Semitic incidents. Responding to complaints from the Board of Deputies of British Jews, the oversight board for English local government ruled in February 2006 that Ken Livingstone, the Mayor of London, should be suspended without pay from his elected office for a month, in punishment for having accused a Jewish reporter of behaving like a concentration camp guard. This hugely overblown reaction, although finally overturned on appeal, is nonetheless extraordinary. Livingstone's barb was almost the opposite of anti-Semitic: he was alluding to the fact that the *Daily Mail*, the flagship newspaper of the reporter's press stable, had a long history of anti-Semitism and homophobia, and had supported the Nazis until 1939.

In the United States the manipulation of the charge of anti-Semitism has reached levels that seriously impede open expression and debate. The play *My Name is Rachel Corrie*, based on the writings of the young American activist killed by an IDF bulldozer in the Gaza Strip in March 2003, is as I write now finally on the New York stage, but only after one of the city's leading progressive theatres caved in to pressure and backed out of its originally scheduled transfer from London. The on-stage Corrie passionately critiques any slippage from opposition to particular Israeli policies to a generalized blaming of all Israelis or Jews — but the show does draw attention to the plight of Palestinians in Gaza, and this was enough for it to be anathemized as anti-Semitic. A sober essay by John Mearsheimer and Stephen Walt entitled "The Israel Lobby," on the power of pro-Israel lobbying groups in the United States, was published in the *London Review of Books* (23 March 2006) because no comparable American journal was willing to carry it. The essay has provoked a ferocious reaction from those aligned with this lobby, raising to a new pitch the familiar strategy of attempting to taint as anti-Semitic almost all criticism of Israeli conduct.

The spectre of a "new" anti-Semitism supposedly stalking Europe serves to shore up the taboos that hedge discussion in America of Israel and of the United

States' relationship to Israel. The media in Europe is dominated by the conservative and reflexively pro-Israeli publishing empires of Rupert Murdoch, Silvio Berlusconi and the Axel Springer company. Dissenting voices are rare and relatively marginal, but nonetheless reporters such as Robert Fisk of the London *Independent* (Britain's lowest-selling national newspaper) are regularly vilified in America as representative of the prevailing anti-Semitic prejudice of Europe's chattering classes. It is questionable, to say the least, if the current massive levels of American economic and military support for Israel would survive vigorous public scrutiny. The conflation of anti-Zionism with anti-Semitism, and the diagnosis of Europe as contagiously sick with a "new" strain of this virulent malady, functions in American political discourse to stave off this scrutiny by placing Israel's defenders perpetually on the attack. The status quo will be safe as long as mere empathy with Palestinian suffering, or any mention of the influence of pro-Israel lobbyists in Washington, can be linked by association to the dangerous resurgence of ancient and murderous hatreds.

Islamophobia, as Matti Bunzl rightly argues, is a much more widespread and serious problem in contemporary Europe (and beyond). For many Western liberals, a caricatured, monolithic Islam now essentially figures as the binary opposite of the positive values of progressive modernity, and it is in contrast to this Islamic negative that these positive values find their form. "They" are dogmatic, fanatical, oppressive of women, homophobic, repressive of free speech, violent; "we," in contrast, are not (although in fact, of course, in some similar and some different ways, we often are). Until the 1980s Communism provided a similar pole of contrast, and before Communism it was Judaism. For Voltaire, most famously, the barbarous, superstitious, primitive Jews stood as the clear antithesis of his own less clearly enunciated ideals of peaceable and rational civility. Voltaire's reputation as the leading defender of toleration was not undermined but underscored by his repeated attacks on the violence and idiocy of Jewish narrow-mindedness and intolerance. The recent "Danish Cartoons" debacle highlighted the same dynamic in relation to Islam. While even ardent secularists generally respect the sensitivities that surround Christian and Jewish religious symbols, an image of Mohammed with a bomb under his turban, designed to offend on multiple levels, was adopted as a rallying point behind which to confirm the barbarism of those who objected to it. Western "toleration" — practised as selective provocation — thus comes into relief in contrast to supposedly Islamic violence and fanaticism (even though only a very small minority of Muslims reacted with violence to the Cartoons).

There is, then, most certainly a strong historical parallel between anti-Semitism in the past and Islamophobia in the present. There are very profound differences, however, in the ways in which these two prejudices figure in the contemporary world. The well-meaning aspiration of European left-liberals, such as those at the European Union Monitoring Centre, to "build bridges" between these European minority communities by emphasizing their similarities of experience is, unfortunately, doomed to failure if no account is also taken of the points of difference and disagreement between Jews and Muslims in Europe. European Jews are predominantly well integrated, highly educated and relatively affluent. Relative to their demographic strength they are disproportionately visible in politics, the professions and cultural industries, and their diverse voices are clearly heard in the media (in Britain, for example, Jews have figured at the fore on both sides in various boycott debates related to Israel). European Muslims, in contrast, are disproportionately poor, unemployed and socio-culturally marginalized. There are few prominent European Muslim intellectuals. Most importantly, perhaps, because of the Holocaust, organized Jewry in Europe possesses a unique moral authority, whereas Muslims, since the terror attacks in New York, Madrid and London, are popularly marked more as perpetrators than as victims of violence.

And then there is Israel. Violence by Israel is followed by violence around the world, often but not only by Muslims, against Jews: this familiar pattern repeated itself most recently during Israel's war with Hezbollah in the summer of 2006. This truth is, of course, ugly, but it is also unsurprising, given the level of disaffection of many young European Muslims, the close public alignment with Israel of European organized Jewry, and the immense gulf between perceptions of the conflict mediated through European and through Arab media sources. Conflict in the Middle East and ethnic tension in Europe are inescapably linked.

There is also a connection between violence by Israel and the dramatic decline in anti-Semitism on the European far Right. Matti Bunzl's essay has documented with great lucidity the striking shift in rhetoric on Jewish issues from far Right parties in Austria, France and Belgium. In Britain, also, the British National Party has decisively distanced itself from its anti-Semitic past. The BNP officially espouses neutrality on the Israel/Palestine conflict, focusing attention on the domestic peril of the "Islamification" of Britain. However, a leading columnist on the BNP website, Lee Barnes, expressed his "100% support" for Israel in its conflict with Hezbollah, identifying it as a frontline bulwark against Europe becoming "Eurabia." It would be very surprising if most European Arab-haters and Islamophobes, observing Israeli military operations in Gaza, the West Bank and in Lebanon, did not like what they see.

With the recent widening of Ehud Olmert's governing coalition in Israel to include Avigdor Lieberman's Israel Beitenu party, which openly advocates the "transfer" of Arab citizens of Israel, the far Right has gained its most dramatic advance toward respectability in any democratic society. As Zehava Galon, the parliamentary leader of the left-wing Meretz party, wrote in *The Guardian* (2 November 2006), Lieberman is "worse than Haider or Le Pen." However, only one minister resigned from the Israeli cabinet in protest against Lieberman's entry into it, and international response to the advance of Israel Beitenu has been muted. Lieberman's party advocates from within government policies what few European far-Right groupings dare openly avow for their own societies. However, the appeal of the notion of the expulsion of Arabs undoubtedly surpasses its expression, and the unchallenged circulation of such ideas in one country facilitates their freer ventilation elsewhere. Old-style obsessions with "Zionist conspiracy" are not dead on the European far Right, but Israel increasingly offers European racists and Islamophobes good reasons to regard it less as an enemy than as a trailblazing model.

The admission of Turkey to the European Union would certainly mark a strong and positive stand against European arrogance and Islamophobia. It would make little difference, however, to these deeper tensions. (The issue of Turkey's membership has raised little controversy in some parts of Europe: in Britain it has scarcely been discussed, xenophobic anxiety instead being currently focused on the possibility of a large influx of migrants from Bulgaria and Romania with the accession of these countries to the EU in 2007.) If we are to build a more harmoniously pluralist Europe, and a more harmoniously pluralist world, we must start with an honest acknowledgement of inequalities of power, and of the urgent need for a just peace in the Middle East.

Xenophobia, Anti-Semitism, and Racism: Europe's Recurring Evils?

Esther Benbassa
École Pratique des Hautes Études, Sorbonne
(Translated by Paul A. Silverstein)

Having read Matti Bunzl's article in one sitting, I completely agree with the historical perspective he brings to questions of anti-Semitism and Islamophobia. He sets out distinctions which are absolutely vital, given the general confusion on these issues which currently exists in a Europe in the process of trying to construct a supranational identity, but where opposition to its project remains strong. Paradoxically, this opposition is not always directly connected with

Europe itself. In the case of France, the 2004 debate around the adoption referendum for the European Constitution crystallized around domestic political issues, over fears of globalization and the establishment of a neo-liberal economy which threatened to call into question social benefits jealously defended by French citizens. It goes without saying that nationalist (*chauvines*) considerations also played a role in the no-votes in France and the Netherlands.

If Matti Bunzl underlines anti-Semitism and Islamophobia in the construction of a New Europe, it is because the Israeli-Palestinian conflict and the aftermath of September 11th has reinforced the everyday character of these two sides of racism and exclusion. There are certainly distinctions to be made between these two phenomena, but I would not necessarily make them in the same way that he does. Without a doubt, anti-Semitism, born in the nineteenth century and persisting into the twentieth century almost to the point of the extermination of Europe's Jewry, tended to protect "the ethnic purity of the nation-state," while Islamophobia today seeks to safeguard the "future of European civilization." The author takes the necessary precautions to avoid making gross generalizations over this distinction, all of which makes his essay all the more intellectually honest.

I will begin with anti-Semitism. Today in a Europe trying to atone for its guilt in the Holocaust, there is no longer any place for anti-Semitism as a political ideology. No politician seeking credibility would dare to adopt such an ideology that would effectively cost him his position. In a country such as France, the memory of the genocide has been transformed into a veritable national obsession. The cardinal place granted to the Holocaust serves to otherwise absolve the country from other dark moments of its history for which it has balked at publicly recognizing responsibility, including, until recently, slavery and colonialism. Politicians distinguish themselves by their (occasionally prejudicial) efforts to be the first to publicly speak out at sites where anti-Semitic acts have just been committed, efforts not made in the case of racist attacks against Arabs or Blacks. Politicians were even victims of their own zeal in 2004 when, after publicly apologizing for two supposed "anti-Semitic attacks," further investigations proved that the attacks had been staged.* Through acts of public compassion for Jewish suffering during the Second World War, and, by extension, for every anti-Semitic attack since committed, politicians also shield themselves from criticism of their discriminatory policies against other visible minorities.

Ulterior motives may also play a role in the "Judeo-centrism" of certain politicians. Some of them sustain a fantasy of Jewish power, particularly in terms of Jewish control over the media, which makes them apprehensive of not acting accordingly. In a country which claims to be a bastion of secularism (*laïcité*) and anti-sectarianism, all that seems to matter for political leaders is their attendance at the annual dinners of the Representative Council of Jews of France (CRIF), a

---

*The attacks in question were the "RERB affair," in which a young non-Jewish woman simulated an anti-Semitic attack on a suburban commuter line. and the burning of the Jewish community center on Rue Popincourt in the heart of Paris, which was later proven to be the work a Jewish employee of the center.

political organ, out of fear of offending Jews. All of which not only bolsters this institution, granting it a legitimacy which it otherwise does not have, but also reinforces for Arab-Muslims and Blacks, who consider themselves to be excluded from the political process, the notion that Jews are *insiders*, while they remain *outsiders*. Moreover, Jews themselves boast of being the "sentinels of the Republic," thus confirming their status as *insiders* and provoking resentment from other visible minorities. Reproducing the "royal alliance," an earlier political arrangement characteristic of the Jewish condition during the Middle Ages, Jews today expose themselves anew to attacks from groups resisting the state. In the past, such a unilateral alliance proved to be more dangerous than imagined. Today, even without the obvious need of adopting such a strategy, insofar as Jews have full citizenship, they nonetheless have done so, becoming thus, despite their insider status, all the more vulnerable to future discrimination. As long as Jews remain protected under the Republic, they risk little. However, with the rise in social status of other minority groups in the decades to come, with these groups coming to occupy positions of political responsibility and strategic power, and with their populations voting in greater and greater numbers, Jews risk losing, for electoral reasons alone, the privileges which today protect them. Having failed to make alliances with other minorities, due to considerations relating to the Israeli-Palestinian conflict, they may find themselves in an unfavorable position in a future socio-political configuration of France.

Meanwhile, given the ongoing Israeli-Palestinian conflict, Arab-Muslims tend to identify with the plight of Palestinians in the Occupied Territories, assimilating the injustices which they face in Europe with the victimization of their "brothers" under the Israeli occupation. The next step of conflating all Jews with Israelis is one easily taken. One must also take into account the role played by anti-Israeli and anti-Jewish propaganda, sometimes of the worst kind and calqued from common tropes of European pre-war anti-Semitism, emerging from the Arab world and introduced into Arab-Muslim homes in Europe via satellite television; also note the role played by certain fundamentalist imams from the suburbs (*les banlieues*) who have tended to include anti-Semitic themes in their repertoire in the hopes of attracting more worshippers.

The anti-Semitism found among Arab-Muslims and, to a lesser extent, among Blacks is connected to this complex conjuncture of resentment, identification with the Palestinian cause, and the experience of heightened discrimination. Arab-Muslims and Blacks face veritable barriers to social mobility in an Old World where a system of social class, networks, residence, and education has come to replace meritocracy. In contrast, in the United States the myth of the *self-made man* persists, and dreams of success through merit alone, while generally unrealized, remain strong.

In terms of the anti-Semitism which plagues Europe today, I find myself differing from Bunzl's assessment that it is fundamentally new and no longer emerging from far Right or Catholic circles. Even if I completely agree that today's anti-Semitism no longer functions according to its nineteenth and twentieth century ideological bases, I would still note that it continues to draw on some of the same clichés of traditional anti-Semitism: Jewish wealth, organized Jewry, a Jewish conspiracy, etc. In any event, the number of cases of so-called "new" anti-Semitic attacks has remained relatively low, is currently receding, and is utterly out of proportion to the panic the attacks have caused among the Jewish population.* It would in theory be interesting to compare these figures with the number of racist attacks recorded for the same periods, but these latter statistics fail to accurately reflect the number of actual cases. In truth, the majority of immigrants and their children are reluctant to report such attacks, out of fear that they will be troubled by the police because of their name or their skin color.

It remains the case in France that there is an ongoing and unresolved conflict with Arabs that is linked to the history of colonization and decolonization. In general, French relations with Blacks are better than with Arab-Muslims, given the intensity of memories of the Algerian War. As recently as 23 February 2005, the National Assembly passed a law whose fourth paragraph specified that schoolteachers were required to teach the "positive" effects of colonization.

---

*Between January 1 and June 30, 2004, 135 anti-Semitic acts were recorded, versus 124 in 2003. Dominique de Villepin, then Interior Minister, confirmed that 160 attacks or acts of vandalism had occurred during the first seven months of 2004, as opposed to 75 during the same period in 2003. Anti-Semitic incidents dropped 48% during the first semester in 2005 as compared to the year before: 290 in 2005, versus 561 in 2004.

There is a convergence between this set of tensions and those which continue to fester among North African Jews who, on the eve of independence of North African nation-states, were forced to flee from their lands because of their association with the colonial forces on whom they counted to ameliorate their living conditions. These North African Jews — called in France "*les sépharades*" — make up the majority of French Jews. Among them, one finds the most hardened anti-Arab racists, as witnessed by the anti-Arab rhetoric found on Internet sites operated by the radical fringe of the Jewish far Right. Furthermore, many North African Jews belong to the same impoverished class and live in the same neighborhoods, and even in the same buildings, as Arab-Muslims, in those same suburbs which have exploded in violence over the past few years and where one finds the most active expressions of anti-Semitism. Since the recent aggravation of the Israeli-Palestinian conflict, France's anti-Arab-Muslim tendency has found support among Jews, who espouse this position in hopes of defending Israel. In this respect, the French colonial heritage of discrimination against Arab-Muslims endures among French Jews as well.

In my reading, Matti Bunzl underestimates the non-Jewish and Catholic far Right's anti-Semitism which has been touched off by the Israeli-Palestinian conflict and which has broken the taboo around the Holocaust which had long served to protect Jews. The extreme anti-Arabism of the French far Right parties hides their anti-Semitism which, to be sure, is no longer expressed with the same strength as in the past.

In addition, over the last few years, the Jewish leadership's contacts with these parties have deepened. Such contacts were evidenced in 2006, during a protest march which followed the torture and assassination of a young Jew named Ilan Halimi by a group of delinquents whose leader was a Black man of Muslim faith and was suspected of anti-Semitism, although the investigation had yet to be concluded. For the march, the President of the Representative Council of Jews of France, Roger Cuikerman, had authorized the participation of the head of the far Right, Philippe de Villiers, as well as several of his acolytes, and later strongly condemned their last-minute expulsion from the procession by young Jewish participants. Islamophobia, and especially anti-Arabism, thus serves to unite the Jewish leadership and the far Right at this particular historical conjuncture.

On the question of anti-Semitism, Matti Bunzl distinguishes between the alarmists and the deniers, forgetting the role played by the Jewish leadership in Europe which has deployed anti-Semitism in order to defend Israel from the media and public opinion which has been won over by the Palestinians as their new, emblematic victims. In France, the Jewish leadership has similarly deployed anti-Semitism and moreover has utilized it to provoke a wave of emigration to Israel that has been greatly coveted by Israeli authorities who see France as having the largest supply of Jews in Europe. Such efforts at soliciting a mass exodus have failed. As Cécilia Gabizon and Johan Weisz have demonstrated in *OPA sur les Juifs de France: Enquête sur un exode programmé (2000-2005)*, the annual number of emigrants has not surpassed 3,000, at which rate it would take two or three centuries to empty France of its Jews. Jewish organizations, manned by a young generation of organic intellectuals, gained a new momentum after September 11th, when they launched a publicity campaign intended to burnish Israel's reputation which had been largely tarnished by the second Intifada. They profited from the Right's presidential campaign which was based on a security platform, and accused the ruling Left of having downplayed the threat of anti-Semitism. Soon after, the Right adopted pro-Jewish domestic politics, all the while maintaining a pro-Arab foreign policy. This conjuncture did not help in the larger fight against anti-Arab-Muslim racism.

One question continues to haunt me: Why have we not witnessed an outburst of anti-Semitism in the wake of the recent Israeli bombing of Lebanon, an attack unanimously supported by all Jewish institutions, organic intellectuals, and the majority of European Jews? According to the prevailing logic, such an explosion should have occurred. It is impossible to account for this lack solely with reference to the state's vigilant combat against anti-Semitism. Nonetheless, regardless of the precise cause, it clearly would have been counterproductive for the Jewish leadership to launch even a minimal campaign against anti-Semitism at that time, given the prevailing public opinion against the war and the powerful images transmitted by the media. Such a campaign would not have had the slightest effect on the media portrayal, on political decision making, or on general public opinion. It would have even probably had the inverse effect. Hence the low profile which the leadership adopted.

In addition, particularly in Belgium and France, the Jewish leadership's conflation of a critique of Israel with anti-Semitism has given rise, especially in France, to a number of court cases brought by Jewish activists against journalists and intellectuals in order to silence them. None of these trials have ended in a guilty verdict of anti-Semitism, in spite of the activists' best efforts.

In sum, despite several points of divergence, I find myself in general agreement with Matti Bunzl's analysis. My main hesitation centers on his use of the word, "Islamophobia," which he borrows from the EUMC's project: "The Fight against Anti-Semitism and Islamophobia: Bringing Communities together." Using this word reduces the larger struggle to one of religion. Arabs are commonly referred to as "Muslims," even when their religion is not actively practiced and only functions as a mode of cultural belonging, as it does for the majority of Jews today. We must not over-emphasize the religious dimensions of what is, at its core, racism. In 2003, in a country as anti-sectarian and avowedly secular (*laïque*) as France, Nicolas Sarkozy organized Muslims — which is to say Arabs — around a religious institution, the French Council of the Muslim Faith (CFCM), much as Napoleon had in 1808 for the Jews in creating the Jewish Consistories. The CFCM, whatever its intentions (the desire to have a single interlocutor, to promote cultural adaptation, etc.), is an index of the government's inability to imagine Arabs outside of their religion — effectively depriving them of any purely political standing. It is true that Pierre-André Taguïeff has recently revived the term "Judeophobia," previously used by Léon Pinsker, one of the first advocates of Zionism in the nineteenth century, in reference to the pogroms — but Taguïeff implies a very different meaning for the term. Must we necessarily introduce the neologism "Islamophobia" in order to counter the ambiguous concept of "Judeophobia"?

Finally, I am less inclined than Bunzl to mark a clear distinction between anti-Semitism and "Islamophobia," even if I agree with his judicious contextualization of the two. It is impossible to deny that the same rejection of the Other operates in the two cases, both emerging from a general xenophobia that for years swept through the West and which continues to rampage today. Neither the instigators nor the causes are identical, but the two function in essentially similar ways and include common themes of exclusion. On the eve of the 2005 French National Assembly vote over the law prohibiting manifest religious signs in public schools — a law which in point of fact principally targeted the wearing of the veil — President Jacques Chirac gave a memorable speech, the main themes of which were already present in the text of Abbé Grégoire on the emancipation of Jews. For Chirac, Muslims' emancipation would occur through the liberation of their women — a conventional defense that treats the veil as the most significant problem in France, as if the approximately 1500 veiled girls could threaten the Republic. The governments emerging from the French Revolution, following the path of

Abbé Grégoire, had also called on Jews to re-make themselves, to effectively erase all distinctive signs of their religious identity, in order to qualify for citizenship. The advocates of emancipation also considered Judaism to be obscurantist and incompatible with European mores of the time, to lack respect for women, and to display a marked tendency for high birth rates, as Henri-Baptiste Grégoire has shown in *Essai sur la régénération physique, morale et politique des Juifs*. One could similarly cite the anti-Semitic campaigns of the nineteenth century and of the decades preceding the Second World War, all of which also claimed that Jews were not assimilable. The only thing missing in today's anti-Arab campaigns is the denunciation of the Rothschilds' fortune, an organizing canard of anti-Semitism on both the Left and the Right for many years.

In times of crisis, France constructs its identity in opposition to the Other. It did so in the nineteenth century, during the rise of a modernity which threatened its traditional social configuration. It did so, in part, through the birth of modern anti-Semitism. Germany is likewise not exempt from such crises, including the economic crisis which led to the Nazis attaining power. One could cite many such examples. Today, the expansion of the European Union, unfettered globalization, and economic neo-liberalism have resulted in the hardening of identities and the growth of nationalisms. This time, the Other is the Muslim Arab, who replaces the Jew of yesteryear. The latest example of this transformation was the law against the denial of the Armenian genocide, voted into effect on

12 October 2006 by National Assembly deputies from both the Left and Right, united not only out of electoral concerns (given the approximately 500,000 Armenians living in France), but also in order to construct a final obstacle to Turkey's entry into the European Union as the first Muslim country. In the matter of xenophobia, will history repeat itself?

Comment on Bunzl

Susan Buck-Morss
Cornell University

Matti Bunzl is surely correct in insisting on the differences between anti-Semitism and Islamophobia as they function in European politics today. Neither is a historical constant. In the new context of the European Union, the political significance of these terms has shifted radically. The historical and national specificity that Bunzl insists upon goes a long way to clarify the present political terrain, in which the old anti-Semitism has been transformed into pro-Zionism, anti-Israeli rhetoric is prevalent on the Left, and Islamophobia poses by far the greater threat to the "future of

Europe" (more on this phrase below). It would be difficult to take exception to this analysis, particularly because Bunzl is dealing with the *politics* of anti-Semitism and Islamophobia, which is only part of the story of their present-day appearance.

I say only part, because the existential insecurity that makes such scapegoating effective has its roots in non-political, socio-economic conditions that have been more consistent historically than the particular object of political scapegoating. Today's global economic competition has generalized the conditions of insecurity, now felt among formerly protected populations in the developed world, who sense somehow that European, or Western civilization is under attack. Islamophobia covers over intra-European class differences with the veneer of civilizational unity — arguably similar in form and function to the intra-nationalist racisms in Western nations during the Great Depression. If we acknowledge political rhetoric as a displacement of social and economic concerns, Bunzl's insistence on the decisive changes in recent political discourse, his sanguine conclusion that the old anti-Semitism has "run its course," may be seen to replicate this displacement by focusing exclusively on an analysis of political discourse — presuming as given, for example, concepts like Europe, to which all political actors whom he analyzes appeal.

Sometimes the most insight is gained from seeing identities in what appear to be differences, rather than (as does Bunzl) differences in what appears to be the same. Robert Reich argued over a decade ago in *The Work of Nations: Preparing Ourselves for 21st*

Century Capitalism that it had become anachronistic to speak of the US as a national economy, as if the entire population of the country rose or sank together in one economic boat, and a CEO could say in good conscience that what was good for General Motors was good for the USA. Americans share this new reality with large expanses of the world — North and South, Occident and Orient — that have adopted the ideology and practices of neo-liberalism. It has left us, no matter what our cultural particularities, dangerously vulnerable to a particular form of political populism that thrives on making us enemies of each other.

I am not arguing for the reduction of politics to economics. That would flatten the analysis by means of another partial approach. Rather, I am cautioning that historical temporalities are multiple, and it is as necessary to make these distinctions clear, as Bunzl insists we do among political groups. The class antagonisms of capitalism are stubborn and slow moving in contrast to the more rapidly changing formulations of the political. Our era may be post-national, but it is not yet post-class. On the contrary, while the dynamics of capitalism appear on the historical surface as perpetual motion, the deeper socio-economic structures continue to be reproduced. Globalization has reconfigured the ethnic specificities of class divisions without eliminating their existence, as references globally to the growing gap between rich and poor make clear. The very presence of Muslim populations within European countries is an economic fact, a consequence of labor migrations. The civilizational question of Turkey's candidacy for membership in the EU makes little sense if the restructuring effects of capitalism are left out of the picture. Concerns regarding *Überfremdung* (literally, "over- foreignization") are a striking resurrection of Malthusian concerns with "over-population," that drew policy consequences lethal to the working class. At the same time, the traditional political discourses of economic critique — I am referring to the multiple forms of Marxism — appear as difficult to resuscitate today, as is, according to Bunzl, the old anti-Semitism. While the abandonment of the latter can only be applauded, the abandonment of the former leaves both analysis and practice lacking. It is not a question of adding an economic analysis to the political, or reducing the political to the economic, but of seeing economics and politics as inseparable in ways that alter our evaluation of both.

Bunzl refers to the complications that arise in trying to map Left and Right onto political charges of anti-Semitism and Islamophobia. I am sympathetic. In arguing for dialogue with progressive Islamists in *Thinking Past Terror: Islamism and Critical Theory on the Left*, I was made well aware of the problems incurred in transferring traditional Left/Right categories onto a hypostatized "global public sphere." The construction of political debate in traditional democracies assumes a continuum of positions arrayed along a spectrum between binaries of Left and Right. But meanings can undergo freefall within the context of multiple global publics, as demonstrated in the recent affair of the Danish Cartoons. Political signifiers, themselves mobile, slide on the global spectrum, so that mapping cannot take place on a singular and coherent plane. Here, again, the inclusion of economic facts can be helpful, because if violently opposed ideological positions are seen to be mediated by similar existential realities, they can lead us to conclusions that alter the political ground upon which Left and Right are positioned. When an unemployed European worker morphs his football-fan identity into ultra-nationalist politics, when a Dubai woman, pushed to the urban margins by shopping mall construction, endorses traditional polygamy as the antidote to single women's desperate and empty consumerism, when an American male, politically impotent within a borderless world of production and exchange, adopts vigilante actions against "illegals" at the US-Mexican border, they share something more than the xenophobia that divides them. All, in response to the insecurities of global change, imagine a past utopia that never did exist.

Adding to perceptions of collective identity the complicating factor of shared economic fates has little appeal to national political actors, who prefer simplistic formulations. At this historical moment, when national communalism is insisted upon in political rhetoric the more, empirically, it is in doubt, the discourse of politics itself is in need of reinvention. That task will be an uncomfortable one, pushing us over the edge of the familiar conceptual frameworks of Europe, or advanced nations, or the free world. The process we will need to undergo is bound to make paradigms of thought even more prickly. But if political thinking is to become adequate to the new conditions of a global sphere, we do not have a choice. So let us focus, not on the reassuring observations Bunzl makes, but, rather, on the most uncomfortable issue that his analysis exposes over Europe's edge.

Much more pressing than anti-Semitism, writes Bunzl, is the issue of Islamophobia, "both in terms of Europe's future and the geopolitical situation at large." We need to unpack the meaning of this statement. Does such a thing as Europe exist that is threatened by the future, or is the future threat to the concept, Europe, itself? Does Europe have any existence other than as a signifier? Is it an idea, or a place? Does it mean shared cultural values like democracy, tolerance, and liberty, or shared cultural identity embodied in only certain kinds of Europeans? Precisely what, or who is that Europe, the future of which is under threat? And let us consider, front and center, the demographics of the problem that Bunzl includes as an explanatory aside when considering Turkey's possible EU membership, what he calls "concerns" over "the country's sheer size and overall demographics." We are not dealing here with the familiar problem of multiculturalism — that is, how to ensure that cultural minorities have equal rights in a national polity. We are dealing with the totally different situation of a group that has traditionally claimed the majority being demoted to the minority within a democratic polity that guarantees rights to minorities, but lives by majority rule. And while the minority of Jews that survived the genocidal era of the mid-twentieth century has been granted the status of honorary members of Europe, the majority category of

"Europeans" — however uncomfortable they themselves may be with this fact — inherits a legacy that has defined itself historically as racially white, religiously Christian, and politically imperialist.

Again, this new situation is not structurally unique to Europe. It is felt as well when English-speaking Americans find themselves threatened with becoming minorities in Hispanic-populated states; when natives of Dubai (Arab speaking, Muslim practicing) find themselves reduced to 10% of the country's population; and when Jews in Israel find themselves threatened with the overall demographics of Palestinian populations.

"Demographic threat" is a euphemism for biological and/or cultural racism that plays into the winning political strategy of us vs. them — and the irony is that this politics is equally prevalent among us *and* them. In response to the perceived demographic threat, Islamists try to revive Muslim law, Israeli politicians build walls, Europeans vote to defend their civilizational fortress, and the US Congress gives bipartisan support to the fantasy project of building a 700-mile barrier along the Mexican border. True, anti-Semitism is not effective as a political discourse in Europe; true, Barack Obama, can run for US President as the first serious Black contender; but such signposts of cultural progress are not sufficient cause for celebration.

As signifiers mutate within the disorderly space of the global public sphere, their rescue is imaginable only if they are allowed to mean what they say. There is, for example, only one reasonable approach to the issue of civilization. If the word is to have any signifying value within global conditions of multiple cultural diasporas, then it will have to live up to its universal claim. There is only one "civilization," the human one, and there is much *un*civilized human behavior within it. No collective can claim to be civilized as an ontological fact. Yet we hear from every side that saving one's own civilization justifies any and all uncivilized means used against one's enemies. Common sense tells you this is a self-defeating strategy. American foot-soldiers in Iraq have shown themselves the intellectual superiors of their leaders in making the simple observation that if fully armed, foreign-speaking soldiers busted into their homes, they would find it impossible to understand these invaders as liberators, as if American intervention were by definition a civilizational guarantee.

But if civilizational difference is no longer acceptable as an excuse for uncivilized behavior, then erstwhile majorities have a right to be apprehensive about relinquishing their positions of dominance, precisely because in recent history the majorities to which they belong have repeatedly used their numerical superiority to act in extremely inhumane ways to minorities under their control — and no sane person would want to leave him or herself vulnerable to the same forms of degradation. There you have it, in a planetary nutshell. If retribution rules the day, if punishments are meted out an eye for an eye and a tooth for a tooth, and if guilt by association is given the same legitimacy that privilege by association has had in endowing the present members of the club with the rewards of past conquests, then whether that club calls itself European, or American, or Israeli, or Muslim, the future looks very bleak and very threatening indeed.

Within a political spectrum that opens out to the global public sphere, identity politics is a shifting signifier. On the one hand (on the Left), it is a necessary and successful way to mobilize collective action to achieve equal inclusion within the greater polity. But as a strategy of the greater polity, it takes a sharp turn to the Right, becoming a threat to outsiders of political genocide. When George W. Bush argues from a national-populist perspective that we have to defeat "them over there," so that they do not get "us here at home," the blatant injustice of that statement must strike any impartial listener as appalling. In arguing unapologetically that the destruction of Iraq — or Lebanon, or Afghanistan — is justified so that "we" do not suffer, American policy is not merely guilty of refusing to accept responsibility for past inhumane acts perpetrated by Western civilization; it is knowingly committing new ones. As for the new accusers, the moment becomes ripe for them to manipulate their own publics to support further atrocities in retaliation, and so our uncivilized human civilization continues.

But historical repetition is not a fact of nature. The kaleidoscope of political power presents each generation with a new constellation of humanly initiated injustices, but also a new opportunity to liberate humanity from them. Progress does occur. The very conception in political discourse of crimes against humanity is new in history, as are ecological imaginings, world health, independent global media, global human rights, and feminist activisms in multiple cultural forms. If globalization is capable of advancing human consciousness, it will be by recognizing that it is no longer a moral option to seek safety under conceptual umbrellas that claim to protect us as members of a specific religion, ethnicity, citizenship, or class — while the global majority of "them" is left outside. Why, then, when the most evident demographic facts and the most obvious common sense argue against it, does the empty rhetoric of exclusionary politics persist? Can we name this political phenomenon and, in naming it, defuse its power?

I am not sure just how and when, but sometime during George W's first administration, "politicized" became a pejorative term. To claim an issue is politicized is now enough to position it outside of legitimate debate — a strange exclusion, that has more to say about the degeneracy of the political debate than the legitimacy of political issues. It is taken for granted that positions are adopted as a pawn for gaining power rather than as a commitment to change reality. Politicized implies the opposite of scientific. The possibility that precisely an objective analysis will lead to the strongest political convictions and hence the most radical campaign for change is ruled out as a contradiction in terms. Challenges to the ruling consensus are called factional and divisive, dangerously upsetting to a fantasized harmony of the polity. The overarching rationale for mandating consensus is that anything less will aid the enemy and is therefore unpatriotic, even treasonous. How do we account for this perversion, whereby dissent, the very soul of democracy, is refigured as its ruin? Can we achieve a conceptual understanding that holds cultural particulars in abeyance, so that meaning is maintained despite the sliding significations of the global context?

Relevant to these questions is the scholarly approach of Aziz Al-Azmeh, whose work takes us out of the model of us vs. them in a way that is disquietingly sane and worthy of emulation.* Al-Azmeh contributed to a recently republished anthology that takes up the condescending charge, frequently made in the West, that Arab states and Muslim cultures are incapable of democracy. Whereas many of his co-authors adopt the more familiar approach of explaining, excusing, and even justifying democratic failures by analyzing the peculiar characteristics of the contemporary Muslim world (oil rents, demographics, residues of tradition, the colonial legacy), Al-Azmeh provides the strongest critique of Islamist politics precisely by not arguing for Arab or Muslim exceptionalism. Rather, in "Populism Contra Democracy: Recent Democratist Discourse in the Arab World," he identifies as a "constant trope" of "Romantic, right-wing populism world-wide" the appropriation of "democracy" by political factions in identitarian terms: "It is almost invariably, and always implicitly, assumed

---

*Al-Azmeh was born in Damascus, educated in Lebanon, Germany, and England, and has taught in Tunis, Italy, Egypt, the United States, and Hungary (where he is presently at the Central European University of Budapest). His insights into contemporary politics are grounded in years of scholarship in comparative medieval politics from Latin Christendom to the Muslim world.

that the state and the group that wields immediate power within it are identical."* This "thoughtless, rhetorical conflation "is characteristic of the newly resurgent populism that defines the history of "a historical mass such as 'the Arabs' or 'the Europeans' as being the natural history of a number of changeless essential features," a "self-identical utopia" that experiences change only as rise and fall, upon which external forces have only "superficial impact," without "substantial and durable effect." Islamist discourse distorts democracy to mean the political embodiment of the "people" in their essential unity: "the accent on unicity and identity is thus primary and constitutive" — which is what we see in the populist rhetoric of George W. Bush. Whereas political contestation is essential to democracy (always imperfect, always changing, never complete), in this discourse "the general will and popular choice are...placed on a plane of identity and mentioned in the same breath as divine will...."

The advantage of Al-Azmeh's description is that it allows us to conceptualize the contemporary political field in a unified way. It encourages us to formulate the political danger — let us call it "identitarian democracy" — as holding across enmity lines that divide us, uniting that which our own politicians

---

*See also *Islams and Modernities* (London: Verso, 1993). Similar arguments have been made by Roxanne Euben in *Enemy in the Mirror: Islamic Fundamentalism and the Limits of Modern Rationalism* (Princeton: Princeton University Press, 1999), and Ali Mirsepassi, *Intellectual Discourse and the Politics of Modernization: Negotiating Modernity in Iran* (Cambridge: Cambridge University Press, 2000).

insist is incompatible: us and them. But if, on all sides, the right-wing populism of identitarian democracy is on the ascendance, then where does that leave the Left? We are led to conclude that neutrality in terms of binary oppositions, precisely the refusal to participate in the mirrored fantasies of our incompatible differences, is the most radically Left position of all.

Can we escape the political binaries of friend and enemy, and will we find ourselves among the real global majority if we do? Moreover, can we take our words with us, so that they are allowed to mean what they say? I do not know that we can, but I know we must try. Freedom of speech is not about "anything goes"; it is freedom to describe reality without censorship, and to disagree openly about its meaning without being accused of "politicizing" the issues. Descriptive accuracy demands that we recognize those aspects of Israeli policy toward Palestinians that have had the *effect* of apartheid, a term disqualified by the logic of identitarian democracy — but this policy is in turn the effect of the brutal tactic of recruiting "martyrs" to bomb Israeli civilian targets. Historically, according to Mark R. Cohen's *Under Crescent and Cross: The Jews in the Middle Ages*, it is true that Jews suffered less religious persecution and were more socially integrated with the Islamic world than they were in Christendom — but saying so is not an endorsement of Ahmadinejad's identitarian political distortions. Ahmadinejad made a terrible blunder by giving a public forum to the doubters of the Holocaust, and it is not Islamophobic to say so. The Holocaust happened. At the same time, it is not the only genocide we are obliged to remember. And if today Islamophobia is more threatening to European Muslims than anti-Semitism is to European Jews, that does not mean that Muslim assimilation into Europe's existing civilization is a progressive or even possible political goal.

The Left needs to maintain radical neutrality in the global public sphere, because its politics are no less vulnerable to the totalitarian dangers of identitarian democracy than politics on the Right. There may appear to be a short-term gain for the identitarians, and those who are seduced into identifying with them, but the price to pay is too high. It leads, like obsessive compulsion, to repeating the crimes of the past in a fetishistic attempt to ban their memory. The long-term effect of this politics is suicidal, as the verbal weapons crafted to construct the enemy turn their lethal power against dissenters within the collective itself.

I am suggesting that the future threat to Europe is not from outside. Rather, it is the home-grown, identitarian populism that appeals to "Europe" as a given and self-explanatory category, a quasi-natural essence that needs to be defended without being defined, because if definitions were allowed, they would expose the racial and religious meanings sedimented in that term, that are implicated in a history of crimes against humanity. But the answer cannot be to give free reign to the "enemy" to punish the sins of the past or the present. Muslim societies are as much at risk as is Europe from the dangers of identitarian democracy. Nor is Latin America immune, or any place on the globe where politicians rely on an essentialist construction of the collective in order to silence dissent at home, relying on a discourse of cultural authenticity that instrumentalizes democracy, so that a particular party or individual or sect claims to speak as the embodiment of an exclusionary whole, the sole legitimate representative of its essential nature. The distinctions that emerge from such a perception of the present might allow us to redeploy the categories of Left and Right on a global political spectrum, presenting us with a different set of challenges. We — I mean, now, a global, "we" that is in the making — would need to transform the meaning of democracy, stretching it in ways not limited to the original, culturally European definition, developing political categories of analysis that do not presume the fantasy of separate civilizations. The irony is that, surely, most of us in the world do not desire a scenario of political violence that demands we identify with us *or* them. We desire, that is, precisely what our identitarian politicians tell us we cannot choose. Crafting the conditions of that choice, in opposition to all partial identity appeals, is what a global Left must work to make possible today.

Response

Matti Bunzl

I am delighted that my essay, *Anti-Semitism and Islamophobia: Hatreds Old and New in Europe*, has created this lively conversation. Not only is it gratifying to see one's work discussed with such seriousness, it also provides a welcome opportunity to reassess the analysis. That said, I am struck overall by the essentially friendly tenor of the responses. Most of the respondents more or less agree with my position. Criticisms are voiced, of course. But there are few challenges to the overarching interpretation.

One set of questions revolves around terminological issues. In this vein, Esther Benbassa worries about the implications of the term "Islamophobia" and its potential of reducing a "larger struggle" to the domain of religion. Brian Klug, in contrast, focuses on the difficulties attending any discussion of anti-Semitism. In particular, he dissects my seemingly paradoxical conflation of "traditional" and "modern" anti-Semitism, helpfully disentangling them through reference to this "old" anti-Semitism's origin in the now superseded creation of an ethnically pure nation-state.

Other criticisms turn on specific interpretations. Paul Silverstein is concerned about the ramifications of my strong distinction between anti-Semitism and Islamophobia, while Dan Diner seems to urge even greater analytic separation. Benbassa, for her part, emphasizes the continuities between "old" and "new" anti-Semitism and insists on the ongoing relevance of Catholicism in the production of anti-Jewish sentiments.

Finally, a number of responses urge attention to additional contexts. Susan Buck-Morss focuses on the dynamics of capitalism, a position echoed in Benbassa's invocation of the effects of neo-liberalism. Benbassa also mentions the role of European Jewish leaders and reminds us that Israel and the Israeli/Palestinian conflict loom large. In the latter, she is echoed by Silverstein as well as Adam Sutcliffe. Silverstein also stresses postcolonial dynamics, particularly in regard to the situation of Muslims in France.

All of these are well-taken interventions. By my reading, however, they do not undermine my analysis in any fundamental sense. And while they could be answered individually, I am just as happy to let them stand as building blocks for supplemental interpretations.

There is one aspect, however, that does need elaboration, and that concerns the political implications of my analysis. In part, this is prompted by the responses of Buck-Morss and Silverstein, which appear to be argued from a decidedly different political perspective. More generally, it seems to me that I owe it to the reader to clarify the political position informing my work. Not only would this help in assessing my argument, it can also bring to light any policy implications that might follow from it.

It should be clear from my essay that my greatest concerns do not lie with the present or future of European Jewry. This is not to say that I am indifferent to that population. On the very contrary, I care deeply about Europe's Jews. I simply don't think that they are in any imminent danger. As I note in my essay, I do worry about the potential for violence against Jewish institutions and individual Jews. But the number of actual incidents has remained low over the last few years, even in the face of escalations in the Middle East. Even more importantly, the political consensus on Europe's Jews guarantees the utmost vigilance against any form of anti-Semitism. This conclusion may be overly sanguine. But I see no evidence that could challenge it in any fundamental way. As a group, Europe's Jews are doing better than at any other point in the continent's history.

For Muslims, by contrast, the situation is much more precarious. And that is where my political concerns ultimately lie. Given its size, regional diffusion, and diversity of origin, it is difficult to make any broad-scale generalizations about Europe's Muslim population. But all the available evidence suggests that they suffer discrimination in all relevant areas, from employment and education to housing. And while some of this could be chalked up to immigrant status, the persistent marginalization, even across several generations, indicates a more enduring pattern.

The question, from a policy standpoint, is how to respond to this crisis. It should be clear from my essay that I vigorously oppose the "proposals" emanating from Europe's far Right. Whether it is a demand for an end to immigration or the insistence on complete assimilation, they fail on demographic as well as humanistic grounds. But I am equally, maybe even more, disturbed by the Islamophobic turn among Europe's centrist Right. In my essay, I referred to Valery Giscard d'Estaing's opposition to Turkey's membership in the European Union, a position that has since been taken up by Europe's most powerful conservative politician, Germany's chancellor Angela Merkel. The centrist Right is also moving toward a more exclusionary stance in regard to the Muslim populations already residing in the EU. Nicholas Sarkozy, the center-right candidate for the French presidency opened his campaign for the spring 2007 elections by referring to the French as the "heirs of 2,000 years of Christianity," a widely noted breach of the republican ideal of religious neutrality in the public sphere. He went on to say that it was unacceptable to "want to live in France without respecting and loving

France," another clear attempt to position his campaign as a bulwark against the kind of "Islamization" Jean-Marie Le Pen also purports to fight.

I oppose the Islamophobic position of the European Right. But I also keep my distance from a set of ideas emanating from some intellectual circles associated with the far Left. For a number of influential thinkers, Étienne Balibar and Talal Asad among them, the subordination of Muslims in Europe is not so much the result of exclusionary politics than a function of Europe's very constitution. To them, Europe, and particularly the European Union, is a site of neo-liberal containment, a space where difference is managed in the interest of flexible accumulation. Add to this a conception of European secularity as an inherently Christian formation, and Islam appears as a disruption that has to be policed violently to guarantee Europe's reproduction. From such a vantage point, there is no great difference between conservative and liberal protagonists. Where the former invoke Europe's Christian heritage directly (*à la* Sarkozy), the latter cloak their position in the language of secular liberalism. But the goal is the same: the preservation of traditional hegemonies in the face of genuine alterity. Redress, in this perspective, can only come with a radical transformation of the social structure. As Asad puts it, the situation of Muslims will change for the better when they have "institutional representation as a minority in a democratic state that consists only of minorities." It is a utopian vision, related, perhaps, to Buck-Morss's plea for "neutrality in terms of binary oppositions."

I am not this kind of utopian thinker. On the very contrary, I see myself as a realist-pragmatist, and with this in mind, I fully embrace the principles of liberal secularism. Not only does it contain a strong vision of social justice and equality, but it also speaks to the realities on the ground. It is liberal principles, after all, that have been mobilized most successfully in the face of Islamophobia. For example, when the ill-fated European constitution was drafted, there was a strong push to include a reference to Europe's specifically Christian heritage. Giscard d'Estaing, one assumes, would have favored such a formulation. But even as the head of the body charged with creating the document, he could not counter the secular principles governing the European project. Christianity, in the end, was not mentioned. More generally, appeals to tolerance, equality, and pluralism have been at the heart of the efforts that have sought to improve the situation of Europe's Muslims.

With all this in mind, my own political allegiances lie with the parties that champion the values of liberal secularism. By and large, those are the Social Democrats and Greens. In contrast to the Right's vision of supranational exclusion (whether on cultural or religious grounds), they tend to conceive of Europe as an ethnically and religiously diverse entity. And in contrast to the far Left's specter of hegemonic secularity, they hold that the rights of all citizens are guaranteed most effectively by safeguarding the neutrality of the public sphere.

The concrete policies that follow from this position are the ones I support. In regard to Turkey's membership in the European Union, this translates into strong advocacy, both because of the pluralizing effects on Europe and the push toward tolerance and human rights in Turkey. On the question of migration and the Muslim populations of Europe, it means an affirmative stance with concrete policies for the betterment of the situation on the ground. Take Austria's Green Party, for example. Their policy document opens with the simple but far-reaching declaration that "Austria is a country of immigration." Following from there are numerous concrete proposals ranging from a plan to make immigration procedures more transparent to new ways of organizing the labor market. The overarching commitment is to "human dignity" and "freedom from discrimination." At the same time, the Green model rejects unrestricted immigration (the party advocates a complicated point system) and argues for the crucial importance of integration. From the vantage point of the far Left, this would be just another version of European hegemony, a neo-liberal immigration policy coupled with a demand for assimilation. But to me, it seems the only workable plan in light of Europe's demographic, social, and political realities.

Just as significant, such a vision has the evident support of the overwhelming majority of Europe's Muslims. In country after country, Muslim leaders advocate integration, emphasizing the compatibility of Islam with "European values." At the same time, Muslim public intellectuals like Tariq Ramadan have set out to define the parameters of a specifically European Islam. Most importantly, every survey indicates that the continent's Muslims are, in fact, defining their existence along such lines, with large majorities seeing their lives in terms of various forms of acculturation.

For Europe's Right, Muslims are a fifth column. For the far Left, the European project itself is compromised. Along with the center-left, I stand in the middle, with a vision of a secular, pluralist, and tolerant continent for Muslims, Jews, and all Europeans. ■

Further Readings

Asad, Talal. *Formations of the Secular: Christianity, Islam, Modernity*. Stanford: Stanford University Press, 2003.

Balibar, Étienne. *We, the People of Europe? Reflections on Transnational Citizenship*. Princeton: Princeton University Press, 2004.

Bowen, John. *Why the French Don't Like Headscarves: Islam, the State, and Public Space*. Princeton: Princeton University Press, 2007.

Buck-Morss, Susan. *Thinking Past Terror: Islamism and Critical Theory on the Left*. London: Verso, 2003.

Buruma, Ian. *Murder in Amsterdam: The Death of Theo van Gogh and the Limits of Tolerance*. New York: Penguin Press, 2006

Bunzl, Matti. *Symptoms of Modernity: Jews and Queers in Late-Twentieth-Century Vienna*. Berkeley: University of California Press, 2004.

Foxman, Abraham. *Never Again? The Threat of the New Anti-Semitism*. San Francisco: Harper, 2003.

Gilman, Sander. *Multiculturalism and the Jews*. New York: Routledge, 2006.

Judt, Tony. *Postwar: A History of Europe since 1945*. New York: Penguin Press, 2005.

Özyürek, Esra. *Nostalgia for the Modern: State Secularism and Everyday Politics in Turkey*. Durham: Duke University Press, 2006.

Ramadan, Tariq. *Western Muslims and the Future of Islam*. Oxford: Oxford University Press, 2004.

Schoenfeld, Gabriel. *The Return of Anti-Semitism*. San Francisco: Encounter, 2004.

Silverstein, Paul. *Algeria in France: Transpolitics, Race, and Nation*. Bloomington: Indiana University Press, 2004.

Taguieff, Pierre-André. *Rising from the Muck: The New Anti-Semitism in Europe*. Chicago: Ivan Dee, 2004.

Wikan, Unni. *Generous Betrayal: Politics of Culture in the New Europe*. Chicago: University of Chicago Press, 2002.

Acknowledgments

An earlier, shorter version of the main text was published under the title "Between Anti-Semitism and Islamophobia: Some Thoughts on the New Europe" in the journal *American Ethnologist* (November 2005). I am deeply grateful to its editor Virginia Dominguez who not only invited the essay's submission, but commissioned seven responses to it. These texts, by John Bowen, Jonathan Boyarin, Dominic Boyer, Karen Brodkin, Andre Gingrich, Nina Glick Schiller, and Esra Özyürek, were invaluable to my ongoing thinking on the issues at stake. At other occasions, I also benefited from input and encouragement from Nancy Abelmann, Daphne Berdahl, Ed Bruner, Susan Buck-Morss, John Bunzl, Ken Cuno, Dan Diner, Jane Fajans, Mayanthi Fernando, Susan Gal, Jessica Greenberg, Richard Handler, Susannah Heschel, Tony Judt, Brett Kaplan, Brian Klug, Lisa Lampert, Ellen Moodie, Andrea Muehlebach, Andrew Orta, Riv-Ellen Prell, Doron Rabinovici, Oliver Rathkolb, Aron Rodrigue, Michael Rothberg, Tim Pilbrow, Junaid Rana, Barbara Sattler, Michael Silverstein, Paul Silverstein, Adam Sutcliffe, Terence Turner, Billy Vaughn, and Yasemin Yildiz. I am also indebted to Ingrid Melief for her generous help in translating the Dutch sources. Finally, I am most grateful to Marshall Sahlins and Matthew Engelke, the publisher and editor of Prickly Paradigm Press, for their interest in and support of my work.

Also available from Prickly Paradigm Press:

continued